SANCTUARY

Also by Judith McDaniel:

November Woman
Winter Passage
Metamorphosis
*The Stories We Hold Secret: Tales of Women's Spiritual
 Development* (co-editor)

SANCTUARY

A JOURNEY
by Judith McDaniel

Firebrand
Books
Ithaca, New York

Selections from this book have appeared previously in the following books and periodicals: *Gates To The City: The Albany Tricentennial Review, The Greenfield Review, Groundswell, Heresies: A Journal of Art and Politics,* and *Lesbian Contradiction.*

Book and cover design by Mary A. Scott
Typesetting by Bets Ltd.

Printed on acid-free paper in the United States by McNaughton & Gunn.

This publication is made possible, in part, with support from the Literature Panel, New York State Council on the Arts.

Library of Congress Cataloging-in-Publication Data

McDaniel, Judith.
    Sanctuary, a journey.

    1. Sanctuary movement.   2. Homeless persons.
3. Witness for Peace Documentation Project.   I. Title.
HV645.M33   1987   362   87-7398
ISBN 0-932379-24-9 (alk.paper)
ISBN 0-932379-23-0 (pbk. : alk. paper)

to the memory of Barbara Deming

...we cannot live without our lives.

Table of Contents

Reflection
On The Rio San Juan

For a month before going to Nicaragua, I had a recurring dream. I was in a village in Central America with some friends. A group of peasant women came by the house we were staying in and asked us to walk up the road with them. We knew the walk was very dangerous and my friends urged the women not to go. I was putting on my shoes to go and walk, feeling very angry with those who would not go. And they were angry with me. They said they were afraid and I was being foolish to go. In the dream I told them, "If I cannot walk up this road, then I am afraid of the kind of life I would have to live."

I remembered that dream when we were gathered in the jungle after our first day of captivity, waiting for the contra leader to decide our fate. He was angry because we had walked down to the boat instead of back up to the hut. We were exhausted after hours of forced march through torturously difficult jungle. I was shaking and crying, because it seemed possible to me that he would decide to kill those of us who could go no farther, who could not obey his orders, and I knew we would all stand with them, not allowing them to be separated from our group. And I believed at that moment we might all be killed.

To choose to enter a war zone as an unarmed, nonviolent presence is also to choose to accept the consequences of that action. All my life I had wanted not to live a life cramped by fear of death, to be able to affirm that there are principles of life for which I would die, and in that moment of fear I remembered the words of my dream: "If I cannot walk up this road, then I am afraid of the kind of life I would have to live." The words did not take away the fear, but they did open me to an acceptance of the consequences of walking where I am led to walk.

Managua, 17 August 1985

9

Sanctuary — a sacred place
   — the most holy part of a sacred place
   — a church or other sacred place in which fugitives formerly were immune from arrest or punishment
   — immunity from arrest or punishment, as by taking refuge in a sacred place
   — any place of refuge or asylum
   — a reserved area in which animals or birds are protected from hunting or other molestation.

Leaving Home

. . .contained, predictable, safe.

Razor Wire at Seneca Army Depot

14

Leaving Home

> Home is where one starts from.
> T.S. Eliot, *Four Quartets*

I Live With Ghosts

1.

I drove back up the road to home
the last time at dusk   past the pond
slated pewter in twilight   knowing
I can drive this road again
but it will not lead to home. Silence
hushed in the fields around me
and I arrived in that moment of dusk
that is like pushing open the door
to a sacred place   or walking
into the center of an ancient grove.

2.

Last month she sat at the table sipping tea
and for a moment this was our home again
as though memory
did not exist
and what was
is what is.

As I drive through summer dark
fireflies dot the tall grass
expire on my windshield
a brief glow of phosphor.

I think
forgiveness happens
in those moments when memory
obliterates the pain and tricks
the heart   forgiveness is when
the glow of phosphor in the mind
dies.

3.

At thirty I lived alone
now I live with ghosts.

In ten years this contradiction:
knowing more   I understand
less. With each loss
I say   this must
be the last   there must
be an end to it.

These are my ghosts:

Two born the same year
died ten years apart
spirit mothers now who walk
where I walk on the beach cliff

One who moves
quietly through each gesture
of my life   the daily
work that was shared
without thought or speech
now only a shadow breaks
the hollow resonance

An artist
who taught me to arrange
each of my days
to honor the work I must do
her days divided
each morning sewing patches
threading the needles at lunch
quilting in the afternoon
at night she rests
grandmother

And when I sit in the tall
grass two lithe brown cats
stalk crickets   and stay with me
if I only watch from the corner
of one eye

with each turn of the wheel
addition.

At forty I live with ghosts.

Crossing The Border

1.

Like an exile I empty my pockets
of the seeds I have brought
to make familiar color in this foreign
soil. Fences and pavement bound
a tiny plot of ground and a bus
grinds up the road only a few feet
from where I plant. The dog follows
her own tail searching for a bed
in the bit of grass as I sink
the spade into the earth. I will
stop here   for now.

2.

Around me I hear the voices
of men and women whose work
is more severe than mine
those struggles we do not choose
but come with the place
we call home.

I heard a man say this:

*We found two bodies
on the first morning.
They had been decapitated and we
searched for the heads.
We found them in a garbage bag
under some rubbish. Now we
can go, I said. No, my companion
shook his head. We must match
the bodies to the heads. On one
a scar ran up the neck and so
we were able to set the right
head on each body. Then I
took a photograph so that
relatives could identify
their dead. For three years
this was my work on the human
rights commission. They
came for me twice. The first time
no one was home. The second
time they found my two cousins.
She was raped and tortured.
He disappeared. I fled
with the help of friends.*

Home. When you go there
they don't have to take you in.

If you came across the border
in Arizona, if you came at night
on foot or on horseback, if you
came by day in a four-wheel drive jeep —
dust marking your trail in the air
then sinking back under the horizon —
what you seek is here
and is not here. You carry
nothing with you. It is everything
you will need. You carry nothing
with you but the pictures
in your head.

I want to say, I will give you
a home, but I know as I think it
home cannot be given, only claimed.

3.

Against the approaching dark
I search for my dog
lost along the riverbank
a child sidles past me
two mastiffs on leash
Have you seen?
I ask this child
no, he mutters,
mistrusting this white
woman sweating
in jogging shorts.

The sun blazes down
behind me and at the farthest
meadow in the mud
of the riverbank
I find people
living
men   women   children
cooking   washing clothes
in the effluvia of the Hudson
this is their home
I realize
as a man steps out
from behind a clothesline
and says courteously
no, we haven't seen
we just got back.
A barking dog
draws me out onto a garbage
filled promontory
and I face in that gloom
the child
hunkering down
to spend his night
between the warm bodies
of two stray dogs.
I thought it was mine
I apologize
and back away
terrified.
He is a little boy
this place is the capital
of New York state
factories farms technology
he is a little boy
spending this night alone
and when full dark
pulls me away from the search
I know it is about death.

She Tracks Toward Home

1.

I watched phoebe build her nest
under the backporch eaves   a nest
full of nothing when the first
strawberries ripened   stuffed with birdfuzz
and gaping beakmouths by blackberry week.
Her third year under the same eaves
following instinct to return
to the known   to what seems safe.
I would make of these fledglings an image
but they leave sooner   more willingly
than I.

2.

A friend told me she had watched whales
play around her ship off Cape Cod one
windy afternoon. Like puppies
she said   breeching rolling
in the wind. She watched for hours
as those earth island bodies turned
and turned in sea froth   so gentle
she said   they never touched the ship
but brushed alongside   controlled
careful.

Last week I read a backpage article
about ninety-four whales beached
at Nantucket   swept onto the sand
a thrust of the giant tail burying them
in air   weighting their lungs   agony
of breath collapsing   all lost.
The whales might have been following
a magnetic polar signal   the paper said
and the Cape got in the way   land
not being a factor which registered
against the pull of a magnetic force
as those whales tracked northward.

3.

I think of my dog
mud tired
after a run
the urge to gallop full out
satisfied
she knows where home
is and her head
to the ground she
swings into a slow
lope heading west
on instinct
she tracks
toward home
and the highway
is not a factor
which registers
against the pull
of the homeforce.

Saved From Complacency

1.

This is not about myth
it is about conscious choice.
Yes the pipes froze
and burst one winter
yes sometimes we travelled
on opposite sides of the bed
instead of seeking the warmth
of the center
yes hard work
yes the cars not starting
at thirty below
yes the two mile walk in
when the plow was late
and yes the warm fires at night
the sun cracking a snowscape
the lilacs in spring.

I wore that life like a skin
something I settled into forever
never saying *one day this will all be memory.*

2.

I wasn't prepared for how hard it was. You can
tell yourself in advance, look, this is going to be
hard so you've got to take care of yourself, but then
there is that gap between what you know and what you
remember to do. And sometimes you just don't know
what to do. After mother died, I remember my father
saying, I hear people telling me to take care of myself
but I don't know what that means. Do you know what it
means? Then — it was easy for me to tell him — but now
I don't know what it means at all.

I decided to leave. No one said to me, you have
to get out now. I didn't want to stay. But staying away
has been harder. In our garden there was a corner,
the lower south corner, where the soil seemed hard
to grow things in. First year we put the corn there.
Nothing at all. Then we tried tomatoes. That dirt
kept saying no. It wasn't till we planted potatoes that
something took hold and grew and then year after year those
potatoes flourished. Living there was like that for me.
It wouldn't have suited everyone.

Sometimes we go out because we need to find new places
to grow. For myself, I went out to find unforgiving
soil where when I make a mistake the answer will come
back at me right away. I went out because it was time
to live without a cushion. Grief can be a cushion.
You sink down and down into the familiarity of it and
when it starts to feel normal, comfortable even, then
it's time to look for a horizon of bare rock and blasted
trees, anything less familiar where you can hear all
the words, sharp and clear.

After a hike in November I came down and wandered into
the woods before I went to my car, not ready to let go
of the smell of wet leaves. I followed a track that wound
back along the base of a hill and came out into a sudden
clearing. A bare finger of chimney stood stark against
the twilight sky and next to it the crescent moon rose
behind a charred crossbeam. Now when I want familiar
things I remember the ash underfoot, the detritus of some other
lost dream. It keeps me in the present. Otherwise I'd
be off, tracking toward home.

3.

Hunched alone
by a fire I have built
on a night too cold
to let it warm me
I reflect
that I have been
saved from complacency
again.

As I doze
from across the valley
I hear a hand
clap three times.
Is the universe
applauding?
No one in this skin
but me, no one
in this tent
and no one
in this forest.

The next morning
down at the beaver pond
I remember the clap
imagine that flat tail
slapping water
thwack
thwack
thwack.

Dreaming Back

1.

I have come to this farthest island
on this eastern coast

the beat of a duck's wings
hitting the water
as she strains toward flight

the scraw of an osprey
warning off gulls

wind in dry leaves

water on rock.

Need stretches me tight
the way these coast rocks stretch
across the earth
keeping it all from flying apart.

2.

I lie on my back
on a rock
before moonrise

stars
like pieces of glass in a kaleidoscope
track across the sky

if each were cut loose
from its orbit
I imagine the chaos

remember the millions
of homeless people
cut loose from our bearings

the rock cold under my back
I wonder if the universe
paused

the night they put that baboon's
heart into a little baby
— heart wrinkled like a walnut —

the newspapers said   what configuration
of stars greeted her first breath
and did they bury

the heart's donor and did
the surgeons recognize
this gift as they lifted

the heart from one small body
to the other or was it like
tinkertoys   a mechanical puzzle

to solve with the head   beneath me
the ocean comes up to the cliff
with a heart's

regularity   how have we come so far
from this essential pulse
what arrogance

cut the cord
let us drift   spacewalkers
away from our homeforce.

3.

> ...the end of all our exploring
> Will be to arrive where we started
> And know the place for the first time.
>
> T.S. Eliot, *Four Quartets*

Waves suck the sand from under my feet
when I stand still and I sink

trying to remember something I have
always known and never forgotten

but don't know now   as my feet sink
the sand shifts into new shapes

I dream back through the opening
of each day of my life   each a story

about to happen   one connected
to the next like the moon-diamonds

moonlight makes on the path of the sea
I dream back to the first heart's breath

past the first rush of water from the tide pool
to the still center and beyond

there are words you must never use
in a poem I have told students

soul   love   and yet I have found
no image to bear the weight of knowing

that home is the place of the heart
that it is only with the heart's direction

we can find the center of that ancient silent grove
or push open the door to a sacred place.

One Summer At Seneca:
The Women's Encampment
For A Future Of Peace With Justice

For a moment in the summer of 1983 the news reports mentioned a group of women who were — we were told — "disturbing the peace" in upstate New York. National media, when they bothered to notice the event at all, briefly indicated that the Women's Peace Encampment was protesting the storage of nuclear weapons at the Seneca Army Depot and then moved on to more important issues. "Culture Clash" was the headline in *Time*, and the real news seemed to be that "the Seneca protest had mainly managed to provoke an angry clash of cultures in a conservative rural community." Did anyone notice that the Governor of New York admitted even he didn't know whether the neutron bomb was stored at the Seneca Army Depot? Oh, yes, but that wasn't where the action was. Within a month of the Encampment's opening ceremony, the "lesbian issue" had become a focus of attention. Women driving up to the Encampment for the August first demonstration and civil disobedience at the Depot had to pass a sign erected by local residents across from the main base gate which shouted: PINKO DYKES GO HOME.

After more than a year of planning for an event that would demonstrate our profound objection to the creation and installation of the Cruise and Pershing missiles, after months of outreach to the local upstate community about issues of disarmament and economics, about conversion from military employment to nonmilitary employment, and in spite of a history of women-only peace actions and events in countries all over the world, the sign read PINKO DYKES GO HOME. So on that last Sunday in July, I slowed my car to look at the sign. It was hot and sunny, hot enough to feel like it had to rain soon, and the humidity was gathering thunder clouds on the western horizon over the lake. The men and women standing by the sign looked angry and defiant and hot and a little embarrassed. The men wore T-shirts or short-sleeved sportshirts and jeans or khakis. The women had on blouses and bermuda shorts or slacks. They held small flags.

I wondered what would happen if I stopped the car and got out and went over and introduced myself as a Pinko Dyke, but I didn't do it. For the past ten years I had lived in rural northeastern farming communities like this one. For two years I had been an assistant Girl Scout leader in a village the size of this one. Our troop went on hay rides and climbed mountains and sold cookies with the help of mothers and fathers who dressed and looked and felt much like these citizens. But in my own community, I was always an outsider. Although I built my home there, I was never *at* home there, never was able to be open about my sexuality. I depended on the almost inevitable separation of village and city for my anonymity, speaking as a lesbian at an event in the city, keeping that identity discretely pocketed at Girl Scout events in my village. So when I looked at the PINKO DYKE sign, I felt like I was seeing my friends and neighbors standing behind it. And when I turned my head and looked across the road at the base, I was looking at my other home, the home of my childhood.

I was a war baby, born at Ft. Sam Houston in San Antonio, Texas. My father was away for most of my infancy. Meeting him when he returned in 1946 is one of my earliest memories, a memory I share with many of my generation. For several years we lived in Indianapolis where my father worked for Armour and Company. Why he went back into the military in 1950 was never discussed in my family, but I assume he was attracted by the upward mobility the military seemed to provide. During wartime, he had been promoted from private to major.

When he reenlisted, he was sent to Officer's Training School in Alexandria, Louisiana. I remember because I was seven and learned to swim with water wings in the pool at the Officer's Club there. I swam in the ocean for the first time off Cape Cod when we were stationed at Otis Air Force Base. A tomboy girlfriend taught me to spit accurately from between my front teeth at a target twelve feet away in the family barracks at the Armed Forces Staff College in Norfolk, Virginia, and another taught me to play "splits" with a jackknife on the manicured lawns of Langley Air Force Base. I learned to ride a horse western-style on the flight line of Tinker Air Base in Oklahoma, graduated from General H.H. Arnold High School in Wiesbaden, Germany, and went home from college for my first Christmas to Griffiss Air Force Base in Rome, New York, only a few miles from the Seneca Army Depot I was now driving by. So the Army Depot looked like home to me, and the people who stood on the other side of the fence looked like friends and family. How did I come so far from being a part of that community, I have wondered. What were the assumptions of that life, and how must they have changed if I was standing here and those people were standing over there?

I was raised in an orderly military life, a life that felt safe and protected. Today that sounds like a contradiction. Then, the military meant safety to me, and predictability. I may have lived on some of the most active — in fact, vulnerable — Strategic Air Command bases in this country. But to me, a scramble was something all dads did in the course of a workday. It was one of the rituals. Like the ritual I observed every day of my childhood at 5:00 p.m. when the loudspeakers sounded taps and the flag was lowered. No matter what base I was on, what country I was in, cars stopped, men, women and children stopped walking and faced west. Men in uniform saluted. The rest of us stood self-consciously with our hands on our hearts. It was a pause observed by every member of the community. In my memory, it was always sunset.

That life was contained. We lived within walls, within fences and gates and barbed wire. Sometimes we lived within language and culture barriers. A contained life. I moved twenty-one times before I left home to go to college. As children, my sisters and I each had a toy box. What it could contain went with us to the new base. I don't remember what happened to the toys that didn't fit into the box — the uncontainable. But there was a certain comfort in knowing exactly what I possessed and where I could find it.

And when I was growing up, the military community was homogeneous, like the rural farm community I later lived in for ten years. I never had a childhood friend of a different race. A few were Catholic, but we all attended the same military chapel. I never met a Jew, or knew I had, until I went to college. Many of my peers lived in Germany or England or Italy for two or three years and never met a European person, never learned a word of the language, never stepped off the base and into a foreign culture. Contained. Predictable. Safe.

So I sat in the car with the engine idling and decided not to walk over and talk with the men and women standing by the PINKO DYKES GO HOME sign. I don't look like them anymore. I don't cut my hair or contain it. I laugh too loud. I make love with the wrong sex. I was wearing a lavender T-shirt with a Peace Encampment symbol on the front and the word *Sappho* on the back. But inside, the me that wasn't visible to them, the me I sometimes forget about was struggling to say to them, "Hey, I'm one of you. I'm O.K. Don't hurt me. I belong here too."

The day before, in the village of Waterloo, I had walked straight into their anger. I was wearing my Sappho T-shirt and my expectations that everyone would behave well, that we might be having a difference of opinion here, but that they would in the end see we were reasonable and nice, enough like them that the waters would part and we would be allowed to pass. Wrong. What they said and did told us that we did not look familiar to them at all; in fact, they told us we looked so unfamiliar we ought to be killed. One man carried a sign that read, NUKE 'EM TILL THEY GLOW, THEN SHOOT THEM IN THE DARK. It became a slogan, shouted over and over, along with "Lezzie go home," "Commie go home," and racist epithets shouted at an Asian woman who walked with us. Other women reported hearing "Jew go home" and "Commie Jews go home."

This walk from Seneca Falls to the Peace Encampment was not a major event. It had been planned by a small group of women as their legal demonstration. Many women at the Encampment did not know it was taking place. Some did and joined at the last minute. We walked through Seneca Falls, past the new National Park Office for the Women's Hall of Fame, past the corner where the first Women's Rights Convention had been held, past some of the homes where the women lived who gathered to have tea and discuss political strategy and draft the Seneca Falls Bill of Rights. About one hundred of us walked past Saturday morning shoppers and a few people who came out of their homes to see what we were up to, past drivers who stopped to take our leaflets and those who accelerated and called us crazy, past the town line of Seneca Falls and into the village of Waterloo, birthplace — a sign proclaims — of Memorial Day. As we walked, the crowds on the street grew larger. Many were waving flags. We began to get reports that the American Legion was planning a counterdemonstration on a bridge the other side of the village, and as we approached the bridge the hostility in the air increased. Cars went by and people screamed "Assholes!" at us out of the windows. Two well-dressed women on the streetcorner told me I was an asshole as I tried to give them a flyer explaining the purpose of the walk.

It is not hard to remember how I felt that day walking toward a solid wall of shouting, angry men and women, how I felt when I saw the way ahead blocked and realized the crowd was closing in behind us on a narrow bridge. I can remember clearly the violence and the hysterical anger in the hot July air, and I could see that many of the men were drinking, that some of them were armed. When the village sheriff told us we were on our own — he had no intention of escorting us through the mob — some women behind me began to sit in a circle while a few of us stood around them, our clasped hands trying to hold back the angry citizens of Waterloo. While the women in the center of the circle talked about what to do, while the sheriff debated what to do, and while the crowd shoved and shouted, I stood for three hours eyeball to eyeball with some of the angriest people I have ever seen. And I thought two things: I should try and understand why they were angry, and I should try to let them know that I wasn't really that different from them.

"You seem very angry," I said to a grey-haired woman waving a small flag. She had just finished screaming that we were filthy assholes. She was neatly dressed, in her early sixties, and she looked like a mother, a P.T.A.-type person, like one of the Girl Scout leaders I knew and had worked with in my own village. "Why don't you tell me what you are angry about?" Fear made my voice awkward, professorial.

"We're trying to raise children here," she snarled, "and those women are making love right out on the lawn. It's disgusting. We don't want our children to see that."

There it was. I didn't have any way of knowing what that woman had actually seen, what anyone in town had actually seen, because I had only been at the Encampment for a few hours. But in her mind, the major issue wasn't that we were stupid or unpatriotic for thinking there was something wrong with what was going on at the Seneca Army Depot. She believed we were obscene and corrupt. She believed we were invading her town with values and opinions she did not want her children to know existed.

And she was right that we were invading her town. Whatever she had seen on the lawn, it was undeniable that there were hundreds of women — lesbian and heterosexual and bisexual — arriving every day from all over the United States, jumping out of their cars and grabbing women they hadn't seen for months or years, and hugging and kissing them in a public display of affection that was probably not common in Waterloo. Under different, less stressful circumstances, it might not have been perceived as obscene in Waterloo.

Contained. Predictable. Safe. That was what she wanted for her daughters. What she saw in women at the Peace Encampment was, I believe, an energy that was not contained or predictable. It was (and is) the energy of self-empowered women, and — like most positive energy — it is, at its source, erotic. "There are many kinds of power," Audre Lorde reminds us in *The Uses of the Erotic*. "The erotic is a resource within each of us that lies in a deeply female and spiritual plane, firmly rooted in the power of our expressed or unrecognized feeling. In order to perpetuate itself, every oppression must corrupt or distort those various sources of power within the culture of the oppressed that can provide energy for change."* Therefore, as women living under patriarchy, we are taught to separate this erotic energy from every part of our lives except the specifically sexual, and we are taught to contain the sexual part of our lives to heterosexuality, to one man, to a few child-bearing years, to specific and limited and allowable expressions. To go outside those limits is to be branded — whore, nymphomani-ac, lesbian are the most common brands.

And because the Peace Encampment did not admit men, that energy was seen as lesbian. Much of that energy *was* lesbian. Les-bians were active at all levels of planning and carrying out this event. So were heterosexual and bisexual women. At the Encamp-ment itself we talked about these differences: what it meant for all of us to be working together, how a *straight* woman felt when a hostile heckler called her a *lesbian,* how lesbians felt about the need to continually defend the reasons for a woman-only action. There was pain and growth in these dialogues.

One vignette in particular recurs to me whenever I consider this issue. On the morning of the August first demonstration, I had been talking with one of the other Peacekeepers in my affinity group. We had been wondering together how many of the women at the Encampment were lesbians. She was a woman in her sixties who had been a lesbian all of her adult life. "I can't tell," she said, with some chagrin. "You know, I always used to be able to tell, but I can't any more." We decided — on the basis perhaps of nothing but wishful thinking — that probably 50 to 75 percent of the wom-en there that day were lesbian, and the subject disappeared until later in the afternoon.

After hours of standing in the heat waiting for the sheriff to al-low the march to proceed, after starting and stopping and singing and shouting and standing still in stupefied frustration, we were finally approaching the Depot gates where the civil disobedience was taking place. Right across from the Depot was a small chapel

*"The Uses of the Erotic" by Audre Lorde, collected in *Sister Outsider* (Crossing Press, 1984).

where a woman had set up a microphone and speakers. As the demonstrators filed in front of her, she sang revival hymns and invited them to leave their wicked ways and find true peace with Jesus. My affinity group had been assigned to the rear of the march where a group of about fifty men who supported the action were walking, local men — farmers and business men and teachers. As we approached the chapel, the gospel singer began to take down her microphone, her work finished, when she saw the men at the end of the march. "My God," her voice boomed across the lawn, "they've even got some men with them." Then she came back to the microphone. "Shame on you," she called to the men, "shame on you. Go back to your wives. Aren't you ashamed to be seen walking with lesbians?" I was too stunned to respond, but the minister walking next to me called out, "I'm proud to be walking with lesbians."

It was quiet for a moment and then I called to the Peacekeeper walking ahead of me, "Hey, do you remember that question I asked you this morning?" "Yes," she replied without hesitation. "That woman thinks the answer is 100 percent." And the whole rear of the march started to laugh because everyone knew what the question must have been, and several admitted to me later they had been wondering the same thing themselves. The answer, in fact, doesn't matter; the perception does. One hundred percent of the women were perceived as lesbian.

To come to the Peace Encampment was, for most women, an act of self-empowerment. It was an act that said, I am capable of judging the terrible destructive power of these weapons and I choose to say no to their use, their existence. It was an act that recognized the power of women bonding together, recognized that ancient and healing power. It was an act that excluded men, at one level, but at another level it encouraged men to make their own action or give support to this action that women had chosen. Some men did one or both, leaving behind in their decision to do so the inherent power of the patriarchy. Men did childcare and carried water at the demonstration and ran the shuttle bus between the State Park and the Encampment while women went to meetings and planned actions and made political choices and policy decisions. As these women tried to create a world they wanted to live in with their children and lovers and friends, they felt empowered. To the citizens of Waterloo and the citizens of the larger world reached by national media, that empowerment was seen as lesbian and it was seen as threatening, so threatening that at times those citizens wanted to destroy it — and us. Because women who are empowered *will* bring change to the world, or attempt to, and therefore such women are perceived as dangerous. And we were perceived as lesbian, even those heterosexual women who marched carrying babies and walking with a FAMILIES FOR PEACE banner.

Our response to that perception, to that accusation, is the key. We must not *deny* our lesbian identification. The pain and struggle that such labeling brings with it is, in fact, a gift which marks change so profound, so life-enhancing, that it feels life-threatening. And no amount of outreach, of community education or class consciousness on our part — I am convinced — will make this encounter an easy one.

But I am further convinced that we must not face the future by trying to play down "the lesbian issue." Women's Peace Encampments will continue to start all over the world, and such a stance will not help them or any other woman-only action. We can, of course, keep our own focus on the missiles, on the protest against annihilation which drew us together in the first place. We must do that; it is the source of our empowerment. But what the citizens of Waterloo were experiencing, and what everyone who read the national media during the summer of 1983 had to experience, was not only a message about missiles, but a message about women who were acting out of their own beliefs and values, a message about women who were self-empowered. As a result of that message what the citizens of Waterloo were experiencing was change: not superficial change in day-to-day circumstances, but a deep-down structural change that called into question the bedrock assumptions of their lives.

What I have learned about myself in recent years — and I think I am like my neighbors and the angry citizens of Waterloo and some of the women who came to the Peace Encampment and left disaffected and angry because it was not what they expected — what I have learned is that I do not suffer change gladly. I don't mean the surface changes. I can move from place to place and that *seems* like change, but as long as I am able to bring my box with me, containing the familiar things in my life, I'm not in trouble. I think that when the people who work at the Seneca Army Depot are confronted with women who want a specific missile out, that is a surface change. When we talk about wanting to convert the Depot to other forms of production, that is more basic. But neither is as basic to the way we North Americans live our lives as our assumptions about family and social relationships and responsibilities. However painful the change, those assumptions *must* also change if we are to survive.

That day at Waterloo, standing facing the angry, shouting crowd, I began to talk with three young teenage women who did not seem so angry. They felt safe. They were out for a little adventure. When it went on longer than they had expected, one had to run home and put her sour cream and onion dip back into the refrigerator. They wanted to know was I on welfare and who was taking care of my children? When I told them I was a teacher and a Girl Scout leader but had no children of my own, they seemed surprised, interested enough to keep talking to me. Finally one screwed her courage up for the BIG question. "Are you gay?" she asked. "Yes," I answered, and they stepped back, physically withdrew a few steps. "Does it matter?" I asked. "Oh, not to me. . ." she insisted bravely, "but. . .," and she gestured over to where her brother was shouting at some of the other women peace marchers. She seemed confused. "How can you? But you said. . .what about. . .?" She stood staring at me, trying to understand where I fit into what she had heard about lesbians.

Later in that long afternoon one of the same young women asked me, "Are you scared?" "Yeah," I said emphatically, my voice letting her know it was true. "Aren't you?" She said no, at first, looking toward her brother. I knew she was thinking he was there to protect her, that I was the one of us at risk. But then she hesitated.

Well, maybe she was a little scared, she admitted.

I don't know if she could see the hand weapons bulging out of pockets. She knew, as I did, that a man had been arrested when he dashed into the crowd waving a loaded rifle earlier that afternoon. She had not heard the sheriff when I asked him if he was aware that some of the men in the crowd were armed and was he dealing with this potential problem? "This is America," he'd snarled at me. "Citizens have a right to bear arms."

But I don't think that was what her fear was about: she was afraid of me. And she was afraid of what she was learning.

I don't ever want to apologize for being the source of that fear. When we — any of us — have that urge to apologize for causing doubt and fear and pain and anger by being who we are and speaking for what we believe in, then I think we need to pause and look at the expectations we are bringing to the moment, peel back the layers of our own "shoulds" and "ought to's."

When I do that for myself, I learn several things. I learn that I am most comfortable working within a clearly defined hierarchy, one in which I know my place and who I report to and who I give orders to. It was a very early patterning and, for the oldest of three sisters, very relevant. I am most *comfortable* in this setting, but I know that it is not where I do my best work. I do my best work among peers, when I can challenge and be challenged, when I can learn and teach, direct and take direction. And I have also described myself as learning best in a situation in which I am comfortable. "I don't like being threatened," I have said. "I'm not stupid. I'm a quick study, I'll pick it up." I have said this in spite of knowing that my important learning has taken place *not* when I was most comfortable, not even when I was sort of comfortable, but when I was dragged kicking and screaming through some of the most painful experiences of my life.

So I wish we wouldn't worry so much about alienating people. Not when we are doing the work we believe we need to do. It is a mark of change. It is the price of change.

Finally, I do not believe we can talk about disarmament only in terms of missile deployment and megaton destructive capacity, or strategic and tactical, or long, medium, short range. To change the structure, to change the hierarchy that builds, supports, and deploys — and may someday *use* — nuclear weapons requires more than knowledge, more than statistics. It requires changes in our human selves and human lives that are so basic and deep they must seem at times life-threatening.

I respect the anger of the citizens of Waterloo. I am myself an angry woman. Neither they nor I could control the final results of that walk through the town of Waterloo in the summer of 1983, but I believe it was an encounter that will have far-reaching and positive results if we do not deny who we are, if we do not deny the source of our energy and power.

Learning To Walk

I have walked myself into a less safe life.

Ajo Mountain

Learning To Walk

1.

As a kid I had big feet. Now I am a woman with big feet. As a kid I used to worry about how big my feet were. My mother told me not to worry, that I had been given a good foundation.

In 8th grade in 1957 I wanted to wear flats and nylons to school like the other girls. No way, my father said. I could choose between oxfords and oxfords — black and white with laces or buster brown with laces. But no flats. Not even penny loafers: they didn't have enough support. I was mortified then.

Today I am grateful, sometimes even smug. Barefoot, my toes are straight and uncalloused, my arches strong. I can walk or jog for hours without discomfort, the envy of those friends (I like to imagine) who bent their toes to get into flats in the 8th grade or pointed-toe heels not long after.

I tried pointed-toe heels. It was during my mini-skirt days in Boston. One January morning I was walking back from teaching class and leaning into a bitter headwind blowing off the ocean when I realized I had only eight inches of cloth from my waist to my pointed toes. The rest was nylon pantyhose. It was not surprising I was cold. After this revelation, it was ski pants and snow boots all the way.

2.

The Girl Scouts got me started walking. I was probably only eight or nine when an ambitious leader said we were going to do the Foot Traveller or Day Hiker badge. What I remember is being told we would walk five miles and that seemed like forever to me the night before the hike. It only took two hours. I was amazed. If I could walk five miles, I could go anywhere in my world.

The Girl Scouts also introduced me to the idea of formal walking. I marched in a parade once and carried the American flag. It was a long parade and the flag was heavy. My shoulder and back hurt when it was over, but I had learned something by watching the faces of the people we walked past, learned something about words I had heard but not understood, like *patriotism*.

In 1960 I was living in Europe and was invited to an international Girl Scout event in Denmark. Five thousand teenage Girl Scouts and Guides from all over Europe and Great Britain walked into a huge stadium. We carried hundreds of flags and marched past the Queen of Denmark and other dignitaries. What I learned that day was that we were walking for ourselves. I was part of something that was bigger than just me, bigger than the United States. The stream of young women winding in and out of the stadium created a life of its own, an energy of its own, and we all recognized it and were exhilarated by ourselves and what we had created in this coming together.

Years later thousands of us walked to the Pentagon in Washington, D.C. carrying banners instead of flags, but I could still learn from the faces of the people I walked past. I walked right up to the steps of the Pentagon where some folks were being arrested and walked right into the tear gas the special police force lobbed into the crowd to keep us from walking any farther. That day I thought I was walking for someone else, to carry a message for the Vietnamese people who were suffering and couldn't come and walk in protest themselves.

3.

Since that first walk, I've walked to show myself that I could do it. I bushwhacked in the Smoky Mountains and got caught in a snowstorm; I plowed through the mosquito and black fly-filled northwoods of Maine. Sometimes I took these tests alone, sometimes with friends.

I chased the full moon up a hill on a hazy summer night, a night so dark the road was only a memory under my feet. On the hill top the wind pushed the clouds away for a moment and I could see the mist in the valley; but as soon as I turned back down the hill into the night's dark, I felt like there was no future to walk into and the present was so vague I could only discern it with all of my senses straining toward each sound or smell. Each step was only one step away from an imagined cliff.

That is what a test feels like. I go right to the edge and have to use everything I know to keep from flying off.

My friend says coming down a hill is the hardest thing for her. She has to hold back because her knees can't take the impact. I have strong knees and only watch for safe footing as I let the action carry me forward.

4.

Walking keeps me connected to the earth.

Once I walked into someone's work of art. It was that moment of dusk after sunset and before dark when the intense light makes the colors seem to glow with their own energy. I had climbed the hill to the cornfield and walked over a tractor road I had never been down before. At the bottom of the field were colors so bright I thought I must be hallucinating. Red and pink and purple on a tall stalk. Walking closer I saw it was a flower garden, beautifully arranged, and these were hollyhocks glowing as though they were sun-filled in the half light. I don't know who she was, the artist who planted this garden where only she and the wild things could see it, but I stared and stared until the light was gone.

This year I walked into a theater piece prepared by the universe.

A rainy day. Dog, cat and me walked to the field down the road to watch the deer grazing at sunset. We thought we were the only actors. The mountains were coming and going behind a curtain of clouds, and puffs of mist blew toward us over the valley. I thought, if it all ended the next moment, it would have been worth the effort of living just to see that quiet beauty.

Then it got noisy. Something was making a racket the other side of the hedgerow. I craned my neck to see what it was. And there was a turkey hen craning her neck to look at me. As soon as we made eye contact, she ran off up the hill, complaining loudly. I went back to my contemplation until the noise distracted me again. I craned my neck to look around the hedgerow once more, and there she was, craning her neck to look at me. A shouted *gobble* and off she sprinted up the hill. We repeated this ritual dance several times. The cat was oblivious in the bushes. The dog sat at my feet, shaking her head in confusion, convinced this was something she couldn't chase or herd.

5.

When I took German I learned there were two ways to know things: *ich kenne* and *ich verstehe.* One, the teacher said, meant to know with your head. The other was to know. . .she didn't have the exact words in English. . .she thought it was more like to stand with someone. It was the first time I realized there was a difference between knowing and *under*standing. I have had to remember this difference many times.

"Walk a Mile in My Shoes" was a song that made sense to me in the sixties. I was teaching a night class in a large city and the students were mostly women in their thirties and forties whose lives had been very different from mine. I was supposed to be teaching them college-level Introduction to Literature, but when they read the stories they didn't want to talk about how foreshadowing contributed to the plot development. They wanted to talk about how the characters in the stories were like themselves. One night I played "Walk a Mile in My Shoes" in class. I thought it would help them understand that literature could help them enter into other lives and "broaden their horizons." Walking home in the dark later that night to my safe and quiet life, I understood that I had played the song for myself, so that I might be able to understand their way of reading literature, broaden my own horizons.

It is a lesson I have to keep learning. Whenever I think I am doing something for someone else, I need to check what is really happening. We each need to walk for ourselves, even when we are walking together.

6.

I found myself walking into an Alcoholics Anonymous meeting one night when the fog had settled into my chest and head to stay. I could no longer see where I was going and there seemed to be nothing to hold onto. I had a knot of fear in my stomach. It was the most reluctant walking I had ever done and I wasn't convinced it was the right direction at all. I looked around the room at those strange people sitting, chatting, drinking coffee. I couldn't possibly have anything in common with them, I knew; and yet at the end of an hour I felt I had come home. I met myself in every stranger in that room.

Sometimes when I expect to walk into a comfortable and familiar place, I am surprised by strangeness. I had been teaching for years when I looked around one day and realized that nothing in my academic life felt right to me. The best teaching I could do was called bad; friends and colleagues, who I thought respected and supported my work, denied me. For years I believed I had been rejected by academia. Now I know the choices I was making during the time I taught college were carrying me in different directions, toward open spaces on the top of hills where the wind pushes the mist away.

In the autobiography of Harriet Monroe, *Seventy Years A Poet,* the editor's afterword says that Ms. Monroe died in 1936 at the age of seventy-six from a cerebral hemorrhage while climbing the Peruvian Andes to see the Inca ruins. She had been climbing mountains for forty years.

I have walked myself into a less safe life. I walk on unsafe streets and in unsafe jungles. My heart has walked me into dangerous loving along the way, loving that has made me use everything I know.

Mostly I walk to get to where I want to be.

I hope I can keep walking until I die. I'd like to be climbing a mountain when that happens.

North And South

Tonight I sit on a porch watching the Northern Lights
streak across the sky. As I stepped out the door
into the dark, a shooting star slipped under Orion's belt,
a matchlight into eternity. Over the ridge a coydog
howls and down at the swamp peepers shrill and yet
it is so quiet I can hear the leaf rustle of grass
and flowers growing in the night.

                          To the south of me
thousands are boarding buses to return home after
the demonstration. I image the departing bustle as crews
take down sound stages, patrol grassy perimeters picking up
trash, arm bands, refuse of this calmer time.

The last time I travelled south like these
the litter of tear gas canisters and bloodied bandages
sprouted among the hotdog wrappers and daisy stems.

Tonight I said, I do not know if I believe in god
but sometimes I think the devil walks in this world.
The words spilled out over curry and rice, splashed
the two women sitting with me into startled looks.
I felt silly. Take it back. Say it is only a joke.
But fork caught suspended in the air, mouth still open
with the words, I knew I believed it was true.

In the afternoon, trapped by sunlight into lethargy,
I sat reading poems by men and women in Nicaragua,
El Salvador, Guatemala. I read and dozed and read,
dreaming the words into my soul, the fear,
the nameless atrocities.

I cannot tell you what they
are doing there, I told the two women, not while we
are eating dinner. . .and wondered

why we sat in this quiet space, forking rice and curry
into our mouths. How does the hand close around
a fork handle as though hands held nothing else,
the arm raised to eat, the eye measuring the distance
from fork to mouth as though eyes
had never seen what those poets told.

As a child I finished every morsel on my plate
for the starving children of China, never wondering how
it helped them that I had more than enough to eat.
And would it help the murdered, the tortured,
the disappeared, if I left my silence tonight, if I
had been boarding a bus to return home after the demonstration?
Perhaps.

But a life must have balance, I hear myself protest,
and know at once that balance, too, is a luxury, like
curry and rice and hot coffee and talk of war and torture
too horrible to name over dinner.

I had heard about Northern Lights for years — once
a neighbor called and we rushed outside to stare
into the black black sky where only the Milky Way broke
the dark. Maybe we missed it because we don't know what
we are looking for, I told my friend.

And yet tonight,
cresting the hill, the Northern Lights shimmered,
a pale green and white curtain hung in streaks
across the northern sky. Aurora Borealis. I knew it
at once and stared and stared. Such beauty hung in that silent
night suspended above the earth, separate, but not apart.

The reason I could hear the flowers grow, I told myself
as I crawled into bed, must be that they push and push
in little bits and finally one push is enough —
that last small effort, no greater than the others —
and the dry leaf gives way with a crack
leaving the bud space to grow.

On The First Full Moon

for Nancy Bereano

On the first full moon
after the spring equinox
the women gather

I come into this familiar room
greet these familiar faces
a stranger to this ritual

yet no stranger
as the sun sets
we light the candles

seven-year-old Alice chants
in Hebrew her own blessing
for the light

at eight we open the door
the full moon pours
into the room

and Miriam enters
skips on Alice-tip-toes
one time around the room

we speak of the six million
recite our own plagues
racism   drug addiction

poverty   hunger   bigotry
alcoholism and more
tonight we will weep and know why

alone again in my small room
I sleep and wake to find
a fully risen moon

splashing light on my face
walking across my pillow
I murmur my blessing for the light

and sleep again   certain
of very little tonight
but in this unsure world   I know

if this house is here
if she who invited the women
to gather   is here

then the moon
when it is first full
after the spring equinox

will rise and broach
the windowsill at the same hour
casting light

on the women who gather
it is enough
tell her it is enough.

Climbing Sleeping Beauty

Today is its own festival of light
the spring sky so breathless blue
it seems new-formed
the inside of a robin's egg broken open
slick and wet
this earth below too round to walk on.

I could believe in resurrection
on a day like this   the energy
of pure light pouring up the branches
of every birch tree   white limbs
unbudded   white light
pouring up into the sky
sucking everything
in this world up with it
no death   pure resurrection
a festival of light.

Waking Nightmares: I

I think that when they slit open
your stomach and pull
the fetus from your womb
and throw it on the ground
you do not die right away.

I think that when you see
your husband's throat cut and hear
the crunch of bone and cartilage
as the machete severs head
from neck   you do not need
to know how to read
to learn evil.

I think that when they laugh
and shove your husband's severed
head into your torn belly
that then you may no longer
believe in god
but you have known the devil.

From an incident described by Pedro Ramos of El Salvador.

Waking Nightmares: II

An eye for an eye
only ends up making
the whole world blind.
                    Gandhi

Declaring Thursday that the nation's limits
have been reached in tolerating
international terrorism,
President Reagan ordered
new military aid for El Salvador
and threatened new actions,
military and otherwise,
to bring terrorist violence
to an end. "This cannot continue,"
Reagan said in a White House
statement. "We must act against those
who have too little regard for human life."
            U.P.I. Washington, D.C. June 20, 1985

Making It Safe For Charles

He stands on the picnic table across the fence
in his backyard. I sit in my lawn chair
trying to write, the April sun full

on my face. He is three feet tall and wire-rimmed
glasses make his four-year-old chestnut brown
face solemn as he tells me

with pleasure and pride
I got a secret place back there, my own
place where nobody else can go and today

we're cleaning it up, we're making it safe
for me. My neighbors have been working
in their yard for an hour or so. After the first

nod, how are you, we have agreed to ignore
one another, but I have seen the pieces
of broken glass and rusty nailed wood they have pulled

out of the overgrown back corner
of their tiny lot, the sheet of corrugated
tin that fell off the garage roof, three bushels

of briars, dead sticks and blown away
newspapers have been hauled out front for trash
pick up. *That's great, Charles,*

I tell him. Youngest of four children, the remarkable
attention, all this activity for his special
place — secret no more, but nonetheless

special, has him wound up tight and he continues
to chatter and I know I will have to go back in
to my desk to write — and do — wishing

for a moment that children had the discretion
of adults. But no. Part of making this place
for Charles is letting him stand

on the picnic table, stick his chest out
with pride and boast, not a single moment of self-
consciousness marring his joy.

Back at my desk I read a letter from another town
about a child-woman of no name, pregnant
by some device of torture, malnourished

as she fled El Salvador to save her life, her life
in danger now from her pregnancy because she
has no name, because you cannot

get medical care here unless you have a name.
And each morning at dawn — *Newsweek* reports —
a family in Soweto takes apart

the corrugated tin roof that keeps the rain off
the children, and they bury this piece of tin
like a treasure, along with

a few rags, some cooking utensils, that make up
what they call home. He works for a white man
by day while she hides in the bushes

with their children waiting for him to return.
If the authorities could find them, they would
bulldoze the tin shack, destroy

their few possessions in the name of resettlement.
Today in this country in this town in my
neighborhood, Charles is three times

more likely than his friend Mark to die a violent
death because Mark is white, six times less
able to find a job, ten times more

likely to live in poverty, to go to jail, to overdose
on drugs, and I want to know how to go beyond
the statistics, go beyond even

the question of how this child can learn to be a man
who is not afraid, a man who can love
wholly, whose joy and pride

in being loved can crow out at the world from the top
of a picnic table. I want to ask how in this world
can we make a safe place for Charles?

In Nicaragua

to die in that place...

MARVIN COLLINS

Contra Captives in Costa Rica

In Nicaragua

I thought all of the children
beautiful with their wide
laughing eyes   even the babies
seemed wise.

In Nicaragua
I was afraid for the children
scarred with shrapnel wounds
a comforting rifle slung
familiarly across chests
tucked under arms.

In Nicaragua
one half of the people
are under the age of fifteen
and I want to know
when you become an adult
if you only expect to live thirty years.

La Esperanza

My children
he told me and I could see
the little one
belly sagging out
from a clean torn T-shirt
are the decoration
belly swollen
but not quite distended
child eyes look at me
knowing too much
to be quite starved
of my home he waved
his hand across the dusty
yard the barren doorsill
the smell of nothing
from the woodfire in the corner.
My children are the decoration of my home.

Helpful Vocabulary

¿Dónde está el servicio?
Where's the toilet?

¿Una foto? No es posible.

¿Cómo se dice _____ en español?
How do you say _____ in Spanish?

Soy norteamericana.

Lo siento.
I'm sorry.

cuidado
careful

Tengo un estómago norteamericano.
I have a North American stomach.

con permiso
with permission

Lo siento
siento.

The Rio San Juan: A Retrospective

I am beginning this essay only a few days after the House of Representatives voted 100 million dollars in aid to the contras. In April 1985, when I was planning my trip to Nicaragua, Congress voted twenty-seven million dollars in "humanitarian" aid to the contras, a bill President Ronald Reagan signed while I was being held captive in a Costa Rican jungle by those same "freedom fighters." Just as the kidnapping of twenty-nine U.S. citizens in August 1985, did not in any way inhibit the president's perceptions of what was right, so a year later Congress was apparently not concerned by the General Accounting Office's inability to account for more than a small fraction of the previous aid, by the presence of much of this money in private accounts in offshore banks, by other U.S. government agencies' investigations of drug smuggling on the part of the contras, or by frequent and documented incidents of contra atrocities and human rights violations.

On the day of the vote in the House, a *Washington Post*/ABC poll showed that 62 percent of those polled opposed all aid, military and otherwise, to the contras. The day after the vote the World Court found that the United States broke international law and violated international sovereignty by assisting the contras. On the Fourth of July the Security Council of the United Nations met to consider that ruling. Reagan administration officials expected "some fallout" from that meeting, but were generally unconcerned. "You can't base what is right policy on an opinion poll," said an unnamed advisor to Reagan. Some citizens who are represented in that poll thought we elected government officials who would act according to the will of the people; the president, it seems, believes he knows what is right for the U.S. and Nicaragua and El Salvador and South Africa and the rest of the world, and he is willing to defend his right to be right even in the face of massive evidence that he is wrong.

Those who oppose U.S. foreign policy in Central America come to their position from different sets of beliefs: religious, political, economic, and others not always easily categorized. I have come to this particular justice issue as a feminist, out of a feminism that moves me to challenge the patriarchal system. As a white middle-class woman I could not fight for access to the white male power elite for myself and others like me without violating the basic principle I considered feminist: that equality for some and not others is not equality, just as justice that is exclusionary is not justice. Feminism has to challenge the capitalist/patriarchal structure that *requires* a working poor population and an unemployed population, because taking white women out of those categories will not mean the categories will disappear. Native Americans, Blacks, Asians, Chicanos, third-world immigrants of all descriptions, female and male, adult and child, who have been sharing those categories with some white women would be immediately and forcibly made to fill the slots.

Writing that paragraph has taken me hours. I have looked at it again and again, trying to remember what I know about these connections, trying to remember with each emendation that not all women are white and middle class, that every description of a racial or ethnic group includes women who share dual oppressions, often multiple oppressions. Why is this so hard for me to remember? The closer the daily reality of oppression comes to my own life, my home, the place where I live, the less likely it is that I am able to see it. It has been easier for me to see what was happening in Central America than to remember to see the racism in my own city, in many of my own daily assumptions about reality. It is obvious to me that if the campesinos being murdered and displaced by saturation bombing by the U.S. and Salvadoran military were white settlers instead of brown peasants, the U.S. government would be fighting tooth and nail to assert their right to stay in their homes. In this country, the white government has made over two hundred treaties with Native populations and has broken every single one. Even when this information is reported, I find it difficult to really remember it, to connect this knowledge to the work I am doing in my daily life. And because my everyday life is geographically located in Albany, New York, the oppression of American

Indians is more distant and therefore more easily remembered than the racism experienced by my friends nearby who are Black. I know racism maims and destroys lives. I hurt when I see it and I want it to go away. But denying its pervasive reality, avoiding the ways in which I am implicated, ignoring the causes of racism will not make it go away.

Awareness of this process was important to me as I chose to work with Central American issues. I was drawn to Sanctuary work and to Witness for Peace (WFP) for deep and personal reasons, and I would have been violating my own best impulses if I had rejected this work when it came to me. But this awareness has meant that I could not do Central American work in isolation from those other painful issues more close to my daily life. The Central America work and learning had to enhance my understanding of what it meant to live, work, and walk in solidarity with those who are different from me. And if I could understand the connections between capitalism and racism as it functioned in Central America, then surely I could use that understanding in antiracist work in my own city.

There were many reasons, finally, that I wanted to go to Nicaragua, that I wanted to see the Nicaraguan revolution for myself: the report that this revolution had chosen to eradicate hunger and illiteracy, that this revolution was working for a diversified economy, that this revolution had women participating in it at every level and had established a national women's organization (AMNLAE) — these things drew me to want to know more. Like many of my feminist friends, I mistrusted male left revolutionaries and their rhetoric of power and violence. What was happening in Nicaragua sounded different to me, but I was not sure how. And yet, when a friend wrote and asked with some surprise why I was going to Nicaragua since she had not thought there were any feminist issues there, I knew with certainty that she was wrong and there were.

In July of 1985 I sent a letter to my friends and family in which I tried to explain why I was going to Nicaragua, why I was going with a delegation committed to a nonviolent and political action. The issues raised by my friend's question and those other questions of priority, of doing the work close at hand or the work far away, were in my mind as I wrote:

> Today is the Fourth of July. This evening as the sun began to set I was weeding in my garden. All day I had been hearing the firecrackers, but tonight as I pulled the weeds out from among the tomato plants, I began to hear with a new ear. The firecrackers the boys were playing with tonight gave a long shrill whistle. Then there is a pause and then the crack. My dog is in the house under the bed, shaking. This noise terrorizes her beyond any other and I wonder where she learned this fear. I don't like the noise, but as I weed I have the luxury of knowing these things will not hurt me — no matter how primally, how viscerally, I respond to them.
>
> On the first of August I am going to Nicaragua with Witness for Peace. I am going because in that country a woman weeding her garden who heard that long shrill whistle would not feel safe. And she would not be safe. . . .
>
> The book I am working on now is a collection of poems and essays centered around the concept of sanctuary. . . . I am committed to going to Nicaragua because I believe I cannot write a book about safe places without experiencing the unsafe places, sharing that space for a moment — in whatever limited way is possible for one who retains the privilege of leaving.

I had, of course, no way of knowing how unsafe a place I was about to experience. And no one who heard about our journey down the Rio San Juan only from the U.S. media could have any idea what actually happened, a particularly incredible assertion to have to make when there were sixteen representatives of the international press taken captive with us.

Preparation For A Journey

Journal Entry, 7/26/85

Letter from Lloyd. Do we want to do a *Flotilla por la Paz?* Go south to the Costa Rican border and get on a boat and go down the river that separates the two countries. Right where Eden Pastora's helicopter went down yesterday, where the contras have the high ground, where the river is shark and crocodile-infested and the mosquitos are premier. It would be incredibly demanding, I think. My first response is to the physical hardship. Do I want to sleep in a hammock on a cramped boat for three days? Then to the danger. Which is, I think, considerable. And I want to do this action. I think it is politically astute, and because it hasn't been done it might get noticed, bring some attention to those border problems.

We did want to do it, all nineteen of us. We were in some ways a mixed group: ages ranged from twenty-three to eighty; we were a priest, three nuns, three Protestant ministers, two Quakers, two Jews, and others. We were teachers and parents and lesbians and writers and technicians. We were also a very homogenous group: all white, all middle-class of European origin, most professional. When we made the decision to accept the Rio San Juan journey which the Witness for Peace long-term team was suggesting, we had met as a group only once for several hours.

We went to New York City for two days of training in nonviolent direct action. The day before I left, I took the grades for the course I was teaching at Greatmeadow Correctional Facility into the office where someone said to me, "I hear you're going on a religious tour of Nicaragua. Will you do anything political while you're there?"

Meanwhile, in our first orientation session, it was stressed again that Witness for Peace is not politically aligned; it is in Nicaragua by permission of the Sandinista government, but it does not necessarily support the government. We are there, we were told, to comment on the U.S. government's killing of Nicaraguan citizens through aid to the contras. I wonder how Bishop Tutu's assertion — that in the face of oppression neutrality isn't possible — applies here. I think Witness for Peace is probably very much in favor of the revolution and the revolutionary process in Nicaragua, but it is political right now to claim a religious impulse and deny a political one. I was certainly not going to deny the political intent of my work, I decided, but I knew I was also going for other reasons, reasons that were not as easy for me to articulate.

Tonight I said, I do not know if I believe in god
but sometimes I think the devil walks in this world.

Journal Entry, 8/2/85, New York City

Kim, Stephen, and I took a walk last night and talked about dying. It doesn't seem real to me. What is more real are the people dying all around us here on West 12th Street in poverty and addiction, filth and despair. But then I don't have someone at home, as Kim does, asking, "What would I do if something happened to you?"

And yet, yesterday Bernice and I went to the lawyer to sign wills before I came down here. And then we went over to Barbara Smith's house so she could wave us good-bye. As we drove away and Barbara was waving, I was reminded so strongly of driving down this same street two years ago in August with Barbara Deming after the Seneca Women's Peace Encampment; Jun Yasuda, the Buddhist monk, came out to the street to drum and sing and bless us as we drove away. Today Barbara Deming has been dead for a year, but she is very present with me as I undertake this journey. If she were alive, it is just the sort of thing she would have wanted to go along on.

I remember that after several role-play skits in which we dealt with the threat of contra attacks, we sat around in a circle and began to talk about our fears. I was facilitating the discussion and taking notes, which meant I was able to distance myself from my own fears by doing the process tasks of the discussion. We were afraid of many things. Some still focused on the sharks and crocodiles. Some were afraid of not performing well under stress, of overreacting, or of becoming passive. Some were afraid for the pain and grief we were causing loved ones left behind, and some were already anticipating the difficulty of coming home, afraid of culture shock and being with people who would not understand what we had experienced. The only note in my journal about my own fears recorded "waves of fear," a memory that is obscure to me today. Much more practically, I was afraid of this group, afraid of being an outsider, which I was as someone who did not identify as a Christian and who had not chosen this action as an expression of my religious commitment. I was also an outsider as a lesbian, but that felt less problematic to me in this instance, since there were a number of people on the boat who were not identified by their "marital status": nuns, single heterosexual people, people who chose not to disclose personal information about themselves at all.

Journal Entry, 8/2/85

I hope this won't be more of a strain than I'm ready for. All that *language.* "Called by Christ to do this work." "The earth is possessed by God and He put man in charge." I mean, really? That is what is wrong with the earth as far as I am concerned. The earth possesses the earth, not god or man, and we have to learn how to share it and share in it. That language is so time and culture bound that it is hard to know how it can still be meaningful to anyone.

All during the trip, in fact, the most serious difficulty I encountered from our group and from the Witness for Peace long-term team in Managua was their inability to remember that not all of us were Christians. There are many forms of spiritual expression I am quite comfortable with, some that simply don't move me personally, and some that are offensive to me. At no time in our planning for the trip did we sit down as a group and discuss the role that spiritual expression would have in our formation as a group, in our daily schedule, or as a part of the action we were planning to undertake. It is true that Witness for Peace asks delegation applicants to be "comfortable with a biblical, prayerful approach in personal and group life"; but such an approach does not presuppose Christianity. At least that was how I reassured myself in the days preceding our gathering for training in New York City. Once underway, the training and the trip took on its own momentum, and I was unable to interrupt the process.

We left New York City early on the third of August. The scene at the airport must have looked about the same with each delegation: twenty or so people and tons of luggage. We had thought the medical supplies we were taking down with us as donations would be weighed on our tickets by the pound, but when we got to the check-in, we were told we could only check two items per person; everything else was surcharge. There we were, frantically unpacking boxes and shoving bandages and aspirin and jars into our suitcases — once so carefully packed and weighed. Some miracle of reduction took place between the first check-in and the last, and everything we had wanted went with us. I was exhausted by the two days of training before we left and wondered how I would manage.

Journal Entry, 8/3/85

Tegucigalpa, Honduras. Green and mountainous. We are in the clouds now, but below seems a beautiful landscape. "Let it be, let it be," keeps running through my head. This is the second poorest country in the hemisphere. It is hot and humid. A man keeps wandering up and down the aisle carrying several fishing poles. We landed in Belize earlier, and someone asked me what

I knew about this country; the answer is nothing. I didn't know it existed until two weeks ago.

I heard a man in the seat in front of me explaining to his friends what Witness for Peace is. He said that we are going down to the border to "put our bodies between the warring factions." I don't think of it that way. To me it is an action, a nonviolent action. But on the river, that may in fact be what we are doing.

I took one step to keep myself safe. I told two of the women that I am a recovering alcoholic and need not to drink. I don't quite know what I am afraid of, but I was fantasizing a time of stress and then a celebration where everyone would be handed a drink. If we ever have to give a toast, I told them, help me make sure there is water in my glass.

Going Toward The Border

When we arrived in Managua it was late and the airport was bedlam. Several other groups had arrived on different flights within a few minutes of us, it seemed, and there were North Americans everywhere, jockeying for places in line to change money, go through customs and immigration. One of the groups must have been the work brigade I decided not to travel down with; I could tell by the shovels and other tools they carried with them that they were probably going to do the August reforestation project.

The Witness for Peace house for short-term delegations featured bunk beds with straw mattresses, but there were several showers and two toilets that mostly flushed. I had never met any of the long-term team before. They seemed tense to me as we wound our way through Managua on the microbus. As soon as we had taken our luggage off the bus, we were told we had to have a meeting. Exhausted, we sat around the bare tables and heard Ed Griffin-Nolan, one of the co-coordinators, tell us that Witness for Peace had gone to Costa Rica the week before to tell Costa Rican officials, peace groups, and the public about our proposed trip down the river — the Costa Rican/Nicaraguan border. In response, Eden Pastora, the contra leader of the group called ARDE (*Alianza Revolucionaria Democrata*), had gone on international television and announced that he would order his men to fire on us if we proceeded as planned. ARDE has offices in San Jose, Costa Rica, so finding out about our trip was easy, as was their access to the international media.

I sat on the backless bench, my whole body aching from sixteen hours of travel. I was stunned: this was no longer an exercise. I looked around at the other members of my delegation, trying to read their faces. I had no backlog of experience from which to draw a response to what was being said. Neither, I could see from some of the faces around me, did anyone else. The question before us was whether we should continue the trip on the Rio San Juan or fall back on an alternative itinerary.

How could we say no in the face of a threat, I wondered. And yet to assume we had to brave it out was to assume the kind of macho, chest-beating posture that has ensured wars will continue. Of course we could do another action, if this one seemed foolhardy. But we didn't want to give it up too easily. If he was bluffing, we could call his bluff. But how could we figure out whether he would really shoot at us before he did it rather than after. When we went to bed that night, we still intended to go to the Rio San Juan, but we also recognized there would be room for change in that decision and for personal discernment; we would not encourage anyone to stay with the group if he or she needed not to take this risk.

The next afternoon, part of our training was a role-play of being attacked from shore by contras while we were on the boat. We were on the covered porch of the house, pretending it was a boat. Very realistic rain was pouring down, and we were all slightly dampened every time a breeze blew. All of a sudden members of the Witness for Peace long-term team who were training us came running through the rain. They threw water-filled balloons instead of live grenades and fired broomsticks. React. We were meant to react, I realized. Several people were yelling directions and we hit the deck. Sort of. One of the trainers was walking among our prone bodies giving out roles. "You're dead," she told the woman next to me. "You're wounded," to another. One of the men was urging us to leave the boat and swim for shore. Trained as a lifesaver, I tried to remember what we had said we would do with the non-swimmers; then I looked around, trying to remember who they were. But the contras kept attacking and we had to swim for it, I thought, or we would all be killed. But no. Another man with our group was shouting that we should stay with the boat. A woman was yelling that we should remember the river had sharks in it. Yet another voice was asking plaintively, "Which shore should we swim for?"

Then it was over and a slightly chastened group gathered for an evaluation.

When we had organized the group in New York, several of the women who were feminists and who had worked with feminist group process at the Seneca Women's Peace Encampment suggested we organize ourselves in affinity groups, each with an appointed spokesperson. In some of the groups that function rotated. Many other necessary leadership functions were shared among us. Until that role-play, the group's organizational structure had seemed adequate to me. Sitting on the porch in the rain, reflecting on what had just happened, I was reminded of another situation in which I had been a member of an affinity group facing violence. On the walk from Seneca Falls to the Women's Peace Encampment we were stopped at Waterloo by a group of potentially violent men and women who stood on the bridge and effectively prevented us from going forward. We had no alternative plan, so about fifty women sat down in a circle on the bridge that day and began to have a discussion about what we should do next. I surrendered my place in that circle for a place in the peacekeeping circle that quickly grew around them to stop the angry townspeople from shoving further forward and possibly attacking the seated women. And in the sun of a hot July day, under the most impossible of circumstances, the women in the circle began to have a consensus meeting, for that was how all decisions at the Peace Encampment were made.

We decided to have our consensus meeting that day on the porch, rather than waiting for the day we might actually be attacked. We suggested and reached consensus on several group covenants which turned out to be incredibly important later: we would not be separated, we would not allow any Nicaraguans who were with us to be taken away, we would not defy a person with a gun by trying to run away.

We did not have the information we needed to know whether the river was unsafe due to sharks, or which side of the river we should swim for if that became necessary. But we did agree to appoint a spokesperson for the entire group if we needed to negotiate; he was a person fluent in Spanish and acquainted with Nicaraguan customs. If he was killed, there was someone to follow him, and if she was killed, someone to follow her. And we agreed on an emergency mode. If we were attacked, if we appeared to be in danger, we would activate the emergency mode and follow the spokesperson's directions. I was appointed the lifeguard because of my training in small craft and water safety. I immediately wrote down the list of people who were poor or nonswimmers, and every time we got on a boat in the next few days (which was often), I checked for life vests and made sure they were with the nonswimmers.

It was still my first day in Managua, I thought wearily as we rushed through dinner and boarded the bus to go to a neighborhood mass. We had been given two history lectures earlier in the day and had gone to government offices to meet with José Talavera, a Vice Chancellor in charge of Costa Rican/Nicaraguan affairs. Hearing his description of the border conflicts — and the apparent unwillingness of the Costa Rican government to negotiate a Zone of Peace under international control — made the mock contra attack earlier that afternoon even more believable. And now, tired in every bone, I had to listen to a mass in a language I didn't know, I complained to myself. But I didn't stay home, and the mass wasn't like anything I had expected or ever experienced before.

The mood in the church was jubilant. As we walked into the building, which looked rather like an airplane hangar with pictures and banners hung from the walls and ceiling, I realized why we had come early. The church was crowded and there were only a few seats left. I thought the reason for the crowd was that this was the church in which Miguel D'Escoto had been conducting his fast and prayer for peace. Tonight, we had heard, was the last night of his fast; after nearly forty days, he was too weak to continue. Thousands of Nicaraguans and other Central and South Americans and U.S. church members had joined in some way with D'Escoto's fast. Some, like the Brazilian bishop who was leading the mass this evening, had travelled to be with D'Escoto; others had sent messages of support or money collected during fasts in their own countries or cities. In the United States our media had let the fast go unreported, but in other countries this method of bringing attention to the war and to the Nicaraguan desire for peace had gotten a great deal of press attention. Long before the service began, people were standing in the aisles, chatting with one another, singing, laughing. Women stood for nearly two hours holding infants. Youngsters stood in the pews so that they could see.

We were invited into a number of churches during our time in Nicaragua and attended several religious ceremonies. Later I realized that the first service we attended was typical. Catholic or Protestant, the churches were always crowded, and the services always seemed to contain this combination of the intensely devout, the jubilation of fervent goodwill, and the casualness of a neighborhood barbeque.

At the end of this service, the Witness for Peace delegation was invited to come to the front of the church. We threaded through the crowd and stood in front of the altar with Miguel D'Escoto, priest, foreign minister, Sandinista. He thanked us for our undertaking, prayed for our safety and the safety of all Nicaraguans living in war zones, and gave us a marble dove of peace which had been carved out of the warm yellow-red stone of the Atlantic Coast. We thanked him and sang the only song we all knew that contained some Spanish — Pete Seeger's *"Somos El Barco, Somos El Mar."*

As we left, photographers and newspaper reporters crowded around us, wanting to know who we were, why we were doing this, were we afraid? When we returned to our house, we discovered why. Eden Pastora had been on the news again that night.

Journal Entry, 8/5/85

Eden Pastora announced on the news tonight that he is not responsible for our safety if we come into a war zone. A Costa Rican reporter called and said that Pastora had threatened to fire on us. Not panic in me, exactly, but surely a reassessment of what this is all about—how deeply committed I have to feel to be going forward at this time.

I wrote that entry from the deck of a small boat that was definitely carrying me forward on the journey. We were crossing Lake Nicaragua on our way to San Carlos, the town at the head of the Rio San Juan. The number of North Americans officially with our delegation had grown: two men from the Peace Navy in San Francisco who were experts in navigation had flown in to join us; eight of the Witness for Peace long-term team had come along, and more would have if they could have been spared from other work since this was the first time Witness for Peace had gone to the southern border. In addition, more than twenty reporters were on the boat with us for this early part of the trip. While we had been training in nonviolent techniques and getting our history lessons, the long-term Witness for Peace coordinators had been inundated with requests from international press to accompany us on the trip. Witness for Peace had been working in Nicaragua for two years with more than fifty delegations preceding us; the press had not been interested. But when Eden Pastora threatened to kill us, our witness became newsworthy.

Journal Entry, 8/5/85

Now it is 3:15 p.m. and we have been in a small boat all day. Between rain and spray, most of us are soaking wet. This boat was meant for twenty or so, not the fifty who are on it.

We are going by Solentiname now, off to the right. Our boat was named for Elvis, one of the four boys from Solentiname killed in the first uprising against Somoza.

A woman from the Italian news team got on the boat in a tight blue dress and wearing high heels. The dress had a slit up the side which kept getting higher. Finally someone loaned her a needle and thread and she was sewing it up while wearing it. The NBC reporter looked familiar to me, and she said I looked familiar to her. Turns out she's from Boston and we know some of the same people. I asked her what she felt about all this. She said she had just been coming to terms with the fact that she is going to assign a video team to make the rest of the trip with us, while she herself flies back to the U.S. So even though they (the press) are saying we are 95 percent safe, I am not sure they believe it, or that I ought to.

Why am I doing this? I keep thinking of the people at home reading these headlines and thinking I must be crazy.

Journal Entry, 8/6/85, Hiroshima Day on the Rio San Juan

We got assigned to our homes last night after coming into the village. Landed on an incredibly rickety wooden dock where a woman was standing in a crowd with a white flag on a staff to greet us. We unloaded our stuff. It seemed like half the town was out to greet us. I hated to take pictures, but did. Wished I spoke Spanish, but didn't. The people, the children were wonderful. We traipsed with our stuff—and our press corps—into town, up muddy streets. The mud was everywhere and the chickens and pigs and shit. I understood in about five seconds why we'd had the hepatitis shots.

Local officials, mostly women, greeted us with speeches and readings from the bible. We sang our song, *"Somos El Barco."* Then we were divided up to go off with families. Kathy, Kim, and I went with Alonso and his wife Modesta. Four or so other people and some kids live here too. He has a large house for this village: a living room, sleeping room, and kitchen. And a TV. They offered us meat and fish and rice and we ate every bit. Alonso came to eat with us, but no one else in the family did. When we went out to the bathroom, it was a one-hole latrine down a long muddy lane, right past others' doors, children playing, pigs rutting, etc. It is poorly maintained, but obviously serves dozens and dozens of people.

After dinner we went to a meeting with the local *comandante* who knows this area very well and what kind of contra activity there has been. He spoke first about how much the people who live in this zone want peace. He said the zone has about thirty thousand people and is a huge area of undeveloped jungle and rivers. I figure if Pastora gets half or even a third of what aid is coming to the contras, he will have over $5000 per person to kill every man, woman, and child in the zone.

The *comandante* laughed when we asked about crocodiles and sharks. Obviously it is not a problem. They said if we have to swim, we should head for the Costa Rican side, since there are at least roads and some habitations over there. The Nicaraguan side is all raw jungle.

After the Nicaraguans and the press left, we had another discernment meeting, which I facilitated. We agreed that if Pastora confronts us and tells us to go no further, we would do what he said. It was a decision we had already agreed on at our earlier consensus meeting, I realized, but we needed to hear ourselves promise it again. Then we sang — "Be Not Afraid" and "Come By Here." I found the singing very comforting.

How do you undress when everyone lives in the same house and sleeps in the same room? You turn out the lights. Alonso and Modesta are in one bed, grandfather in the next, teenage son in the far corner, Kathy and Kim next to him in a double bed, Maria, a friend of the family who lives here, is in the other corner, and I am tucked right over here by the chicken roost. The chickens were still pecking around the dirt floor when I got into bed, but I slept like a log until the rooster crowed at 3:00 a.m.

We left the house at five-thirty this morning to start down the river to El Castillo, the village where the river becomes the border with Costa Rica. At El Castillo the entire town of about one thousand people turned out to meet us. We got sung to by the Catholic church, the Protestant church, the infant school, and the older school. It was an incredible scene. Whatever happens now, it has been worth it.

The Rio San Juan

It has been worth it. I look at those words today as I write and know they are true. The village of El Castillo touched my heart in a deep and significant way. These people lived in a war zone. Their village had been shelled, attacked; their people — their best people, their teachers and health workers — had been kidnapped by U.S.-backed and instigated contras. And they welcomed us with food and beverage, commodities so scarce we knew they were giving us a small fortune. Yet we couldn't say no, we couldn't say we wanted them to save it for their children. I took many pictures of the children of El Castillo, their clear eyes and joyful faces drawing me back to the camera lens again and again.

I stopped writing in my journal then because it was dark. We had been on the Rio San Juan all afternoon without incident. We had stopped at the first Costa Rican guard station we had seen, but the guards there wouldn't come down to talk with us and waved us away with their machine guns. I could feel the tension in my shoulders, sense it mounting in the rest of the group at this rebuff, but we left a bouquet of flowers on the river bank for them with a note saying the flowers had been given to us by the school children of El Castillo who want peace for their village. At the second Costa Rican guard station the international press had managed to create a presence, and so we were allowed to land and sing *"Somos El Barco"* and give our flowers to the guards in person.

Just before Boca San Carlos, the second Costa Rican stop, we passed the hulk of a Red Cross ship, the *Braemen*. It had been a gift from West Germany to the islands of Solentiname, intended to ferry the ill or pregnant from the islands, where there were no medical services, over to the town of San Carlos where there was a hospital. As it was going up the river to its destination, it was attacked and destroyed by contras; several of the men bringing it in had been killed. The Red Cross was clearly visible on the hull and on the smokestack of the boat. We had a brief memorial service as our boat went on down the river. We paused again further down the river to commemorate the lives of two Costa Rican guards who had been killed at Las Cruces in May. This was the event which had caused a complete breach in Costa Rican/Nicaraguan relations. The Costa Ricans claimed the Sandinistas had fired across the river, killing two guards. The Nicaraguans had denied the charges and invited the Organization of American States to investigate the incident. The O.A.S. found that the shots had been fired from within Costa Rica and, although they did not say who had fired the shots, they acknowledged it had "probably" not been the Sandinistas. The press on the boat with us speculated that contras fleeing a Sandinista sweep had crossed the river, surprised the Costa Ricans, found themselves under fire from two directions, and fought back.

In contrast to our first encounter with Costa Ricans, the feeling at the second Costa Rican guard station, Boca San Carlos, was fairly relaxed. The press corps accompanying us seemed to know all the press people on shore and they shared cigarettes and information. There had been fighting further down the river, the Costa Rican guard indicated. Earlier that day they had heard firing. We weren't going much further, we said, only to La Penca, then we would turn around and head back, coming as far as the daylight would allow. The Costa Rican guards invited us to tie up at Boca San Carlos, a suggestion we heard with much relief. We were prepared to spend the night unprotected, tied up to a jungle bank; but we knew the danger of contra attack was greatly increased when we were in such a vulnerable position, and so we told the Costa Ricans to expect us back before dark.

La Penca was a Sandinista outpost. It had been Eden Pastora's base camp during the few short months he was able to hold any territory inside Nicaragua. The Sandinistas had taken the area earlier in the year. In July, Pastora's helicopter had gone down in the jungle around La Penca, but he had escaped and recuperated in a Costa Rican hospital. When we docked at La Penca on the Nicaraguan side of the river, the press leaped from the boat and scrambled up the bank. I asked later what all the activity had been about. One of them told me the Costa Rican newspapers had reported that the Sandinistas were building a major airstrip at La Penca which would threaten Costa Rican neutrality. Was there an airstrip, I asked. None, I was told, not a trace.

The stay at La Penca was short. It was getting late, and in the jungle at this time of year, dark comes quickly. Our boat — an old cattle barge that had been used to take livestock and produce to market — had no lights. The river was treacherous in places and going back upstream was much slower. We wanted to reach Boca San Carlos before dark, so we sang a quick *"Somos El Barco"* and waved good-bye. The Sandinista soldiers, some of them looking like the young teenage boys they were, returned our song with a hymn.

We tied up at Boca San Carlos and began to fix dinner. The mood on the boat was subdued, but optimistic. Pastora had not tried to stop us from making the trip. We had gone to La Penca, and we thought if he had been serious about his threat, he would have tried to prevent us from going that far. The Costa Ricans seemed to be friendly; we knew that they could have been a problem. Two weeks before the *Village Voice* had carried an article about how the Costa Rican guard in this area supported the contras, moved freely in and out of the contra base camps. When several U.S. mercenaries were arrested by Costa Rican guards in a contra camp on the Costa Rican side of the border, the mercenaries were surprised: they thought the Costa Ricans were coming to visit, as they had done frequently before.

After some rice and beans prepared by one of the Nicaraguan crew women, we began to string up hammocks. The barge was small — about twelve feet wide and fifty feet long — and there was no way fifty people were going to be able to sleep in that amount of floor space. Our solution was two layers of hammocks and one level of floor pads. I climbed into a hammock on the top level with a little help from my friends and watched people arrange themselves around and under me. I prayed for good bladder control, as I realized what it was going to take to get out of the hammock in the middle of the night.

Suddenly there were voices shouting up on the bank. Some reporters had gone up on the bank and they came sliding down to the boat followed by the Costa Rican guard who told us we could not tie up there for the night. We must leave immediately. Sensing danger, we were automatically in the emergency mode and our negotiator spoke with the guard. But the guard was adamant. He had his orders. And he had his machine gun. The captain of the boat protested he had no lights and we were near rapids; it was very dangerous to move. Why hadn't the guard told us to move in the daylight? But he had his orders, and it became clear we must cross the river and tie up on the Nicaraguan side. Most of us stayed where we were. A few on the ground floor level got the strongest flashlights from the group and the captain started the engines. I swung in my hammock as we began to move, sure that we were being set up, sure the Costa Rican guard and the contras had arranged this and we would be attacked during the night. Perhaps the contras were on the other shore waiting for us. There was no way we could hide. Terrified, realizing that — hung high in my hammock — I was totally vulnerable to a stray gunshot or to shrapnel or grenade fragments, I fell sound asleep.

And woke to the most beautiful dawn I have ever seen. The light was just beginning at 5:30 a.m. as I opened my eyes and realized where I was, recaptured for a moment the fear with which I had slept, and realized I had lived through the night. The mist was drifting up off a wide expanse of slate blue water and the hills were a deep black-green. Every moment the colors changed as the sun climbed higher.

Journal Entry, 8/7/85, on the Rio San Juan

We are alive. It is 7:45 a.m. and they say contra attacks generally end by about 8:00. Last night we docked back at Boca San Carlos, but after dark the Costa Ricans asked us to leave. We refused at first, sure the Civil Guard and ARDE...

9:38 a.m.

Well, a gunshot stopped that. We all hit the deck and stayed down until they told us to disembark. When we went down, Kathy and I hit heads and I thought I was hurt, but apparently they fired overhead. We got off the boat just like we had agreed, by affinity groups. They lined us up on the bank — all the TV cameras were rolling. We negotiated. They searched the boat — for arms, I guess. The two women and the baby and the rest of the Nicaraguan crew came along. We were marched for over an hour in mud and roots. I wasn't sure everyone would make it, but we did. Some wearing sandals were barefoot after a short distance.

I was wearing my extra-tight-lacing Nike jogging shoes and still found it hard. I can only imagine what it was like barefoot.

They were the contras, armed men, part of Eden Pastora's group ARDE. They fired a warning shot over the bow of our boat and ordered us to shore. Because of our previous consensus, that we would not try to run from someone who was armed, we knew immediately what to do and told the captain to put into shore as the gunmen had indicated. We had not been fired on wantonly, had not been wounded or killed, which gave us a certain optimism as we entered this very dangerous situation. But we were surrounded by men with rifles and machetes, men whose leader had said he would order them to kill us, and so we carried ourselves carefully, fearfully and — almost always — calmly during the time of the capture. I took notes in my journal every chance I had.

1:15 p.m.

We are at a hut with a thatched roof. When we stopped on the last hill before we got here and took time for a prayer, I felt the fear — then and on the boat when we heard the shot. Now people are singing and we all know we got a radio message out to WFP in Manugua saying we had been taken. The captain of the boat says we are officially hostages since we have been brought here illegally to Costa Rica.

Some leader is supposed to come and talk to us, but he can't get here until 3:00 p.m. So we may be spending the night since it gets dark at 6:00 p.m., and we are more hours than that away from El Castillo. Some of the long-term staff are joking, saying things like "This group gets *everything*," and we answer, "We want to know why this meeting wasn't on the agenda." But for all the joking, it is more like the night that my dog got killed. That gradual realization that my plans aren't mine any more, that this thing isn't in our control, and that this action's outcome could be anything.

I don't feel at all secure, since I think part of this was planned in Washington. The central WFP office sent out a press release yesterday saying if we were in danger from U.S.-backed and funded contras, then they were holding Reagan personally responsible.

Just noticed two children who weren't visible before — a girl about ten and a boy, four or so. They are watching Moira and one of the reporters dance while some of the group are singing and clapping. There is a dog and a chicken. The contras said they had only been here a couple of hours waiting for us, but they clearly live here and want us to think they operate on the Nicaraguan side. Another young boy just appeared. I wonder how many people do live here and whether they realize we may all be staying here too. . .with the mosquitos, fleas, and chicken shit.

So I am sitting in the sun for a moment, wet and steaming, writing this and listening to these incredible jungle noises rising from the valley, nearly directly below me. Two boys are carrying a huge pail of water up the slope, which is a rank, slippery, red mud. The noise of the stream and the constant surge of something like cicadas, and an occasional bird. It is beautiful. But where are the roads? How do people live here? Especially if they can't use the river for travel.

This slope has been cleared. There is cow shit around. The heat is so intense right now. I look at these men and wonder if they could really kill us if the leader tells them to. And then I know that is a foolish question. Who are we to them? They have killed unarmed people before.

As time wore on at the hut and water ran low and it became clear that there was no food and that we were not going to be able to leave that day, even if the leader should want to free us when he arrived, our negotiator asked permission for us to go down to the boat to spend the night. There was water there, and some of us had medications on the boat. We could not have arranged to sleep at all in the twenty-by-twenty-foot space available under the thatched roof of the hut porch. Yes, he said, we could go to the boat. Buoyed by this compromise, we set out to retrace our steps. We were very aware now who among us was having difficulty with the terrain, and we were careful not to set a pace any faster than our slowest person could maintain. As usual, the press corps pushed ahead to get shots of us coming through the mud, and then they went on to get back to the boat. I do not know if they were accompanied by contras at that time. I do know they took the wrong path to go to the boat and no one stopped them or questioned them. We followed. For over an hour we fought our way up and down hills in mud up to our knees. Finally, William, the contras' local leader, came racing up behind us and told us we were on the wrong path and had to retrace our steps — almost the whole way back to the hut where we had taken a wrong fork. The heavy woman who was having the most trouble in the mud and with the hills, falling, crawling on her belly when the people on either side of her could not sustain her, turned to me and asked, with the high pitch of hysteria in her voice, "Judith, are they torturing us?" And for her, it was torture.

When we came back to the place where we had taken the wrong path, the contra leader — angered, it seemed, that we had gotten out of his control — ordered us to return to the hut. Then he went back down the path to find the press corps who had gone much further out of the way than we had. In a moment, we decided not to obey that order and turned and went down toward the river. We got within about 600 feet of the boat when he caught up with us again. We were right by the river in a cocoa grove resting. Two people were lying on the ground, literally unable to crawl any further. Now he was furious that we had disobeyed his order. He marched between the grove and the boat, swinging his machete. He shouted that we were to get up and climb back up to the hut.

We knew his command was not rational. It would be dark in another fifteen minutes. Even with stretchers, it was not clear we could all make the climb again. Our negotiator suggested we keep very still. We surrounded the two people lying on the ground and sang softly. I was fairly sure we would be killed, that he would try to kill the two people who couldn't keep up with us, and we would refuse to be separated, and we would all be killed.

My body was not entirely under my control, I noticed at that time. It was shaking and I was crying. And at that moment a voice inside me said, rather sternly, "All right, McDaniel. You got yourself here. Now you'd better see how you feel about it." And I did. And I felt fine. To die in that place, having come there for the reason I had come, did not seem the most terrible thing to me then. I also remember feeling very tired, not only the tiredness that came with the physical and emotional fatigue of the last few hours or days, but a larger tiredness in my soul. I had worked so hard for so long for change, change that seemed ephemeral in that moment. If I died here, others could work and I could rest. And for two years I had lived and worked without an emotional partner in my personal life; I was tired of being lonely. I did not *want* to die, but in that moment I accepted the possibility of my own death, not nobly and selflessly, but as a possible extension of the changes I had been experiencing.

The contra leader calmed down. He told us to get on the boat. There would be no lights, no talk, no food. If the Sandinistas came to save us, he said, "Your lives will be as nothing." That night I lay in my hammock again and listened to the radio operator send a message to Managua. He sent it over and over again because the battery was very weak: *"No nos salven, no nos salven."* Don't save us. Don't save us. And from up on the bank where the contras guarding the boat stood, I could hear the strains of a song coming from a radio they had borrowed from one of the reporters. The song was "We Are the World."

Journal Entry, 8/8/85, Rio San Juan

Another gorgeous morning — we survived another night. Now Julie is playing the guitar and one of the contras, Israel, is on board waiting for us to charge the battery enough to send a radio message to Managua. He is sitting between two American women who speak Spanish, and I saw him writing something down for one of them. A reporter for a Nicaraguan newspaper talked to one of the contras who said he was nineteen and had been fighting for four years. It is an awful life, he says. He asked about the Amnesty — the Sandinista's promise that any contra can come home and be given complete immunity — said he knew some men who had gone back under it and been killed. I asked if that could be true. The reporter said no, she would have heard about it.

The leader who was so upset last night is named William. He says he was a small "rancher" and has been fighting for three years. He said that the Sandinistas had meetings all the time and wanted him to do group projects. It is hard to believe someone would kill over that. I'm sure the other reason is the violence. All these places along the river have been abandoned and what happened to us yesterday is why. They have this wonderful waterway for access and can't use it.

Last night at nine-thirty on a Bolivian radio station we heard that we were being held hostage in Costa Rica and the Nicaraguan government had suggested that the U.S. negotiate with Costa Rica directly for our release. This morning we heard Costa Rica say they had searched for us and we weren't here, that it was all a Sandinista propaganda stunt. This boat is large and there is only one Rio San Juan and we are very visible on it if a plane or helicopter bothered to fly up the river. We could die here, a figment of someone's imagination.

10:35 a.m.

Well, now ARDE says on Costa Rican radio that they have us and they will turn us over to Costa Rica. Stranger and stranger. How could they do that? It would implicate Costa Rica directly.

About eleven-thirty in the morning, there was sudden activity up on the bank. Several of the contra guards came down and ordered us off the boat and back up in the jungle. The leader had come. We asked if he would come on the boat and meet with us, but that was not possible. And so all of us but the two who were sick with exhaustion went back up on shore to the cocoa grove where we had been the night before. Would they shoot us now, I wondered, if the order was given. Mary told me that what I had seen Israel writing was a letter to his mother in Blue Fields, a town on the Nicaraguan Atlantic Coast. He had not seen her or communicated with her in three years and Mary said she would have a Witness for Peace person take it to his mother. Would he shoot her?

As we filed into the grove, unsure what would happen but less afraid than the night before, a slim man with a moustache who looked about thirty was waiting for us. If this was the leader we were waiting for, it certainly wasn't Eden Pastora. He looked each of us in the face, and when he began speaking it was to say, "Oh, I see some familiar faces here." He meant the Nicaraguan crew, and he called some of them by name and said who their brothers or mothers were. It was clearly meant to be intimidating and we were careful to keep them in our midst in case he decided to separate them from us. We knew they were more at risk than we. He then told us his name was Daniel and he was not from ARDE but from an independent Christian group fighting the communists in Nicaragua. I was astonished. How could he not be from ARDE? All of these men had said they were from ARDE, talked about Pastora as their leader, talked about the military structure of ARDE, how many units there were, and so forth. Then I realized the lie. Of course. No one was going to take responsibility for our kidnapping. Costa Rica must have reacted to the news broadcast that ARDE was turning us over to them. And I knew ARDE was going to receive some of the $27 million voted to the contras by Congress in April. It wouldn't look good for them to be holding U.S. hostages when the money was divided.

And then we were released. On the way back to the boat, the crew members told us they knew this "Daniel" very well. Of course he was from ARDE. His real name, they told us, was Noel Boniche and he had lived in Solentiname before he stole some project money from the village there and went off to join ARDE. Later we saw a photograph of him with several other men in uniform and an ARDE patch on his clothing. It didn't seem to matter that much then in the cocoa grove as we were walking toward the boat. We had been told we could resume our journey and we wanted to leave quickly so that we could be back in El Castillo before dark.

The Lifetime Of A Lie

About a half hour after we were headed back up the river, a helicopter flew over us, then landed on the bank just ahead of us. A Costa Rican officer waved us to shore. We obeyed the summons, even though we were concerned about time. His name was Colonel Chavez and he told us he had been searching for us since the day before. We did not tell him how surprised we were to hear this since our boat had been in clear view of his helicopter any time in the last twenty-nine hours. Nor did we say how surprised we were that he found us so shortly after our release, that it seemed to us the contras must have notified him it was all right for him to search for us now. We did tell him exactly what had happened and where we had been, and we gave him a description of all of our captors and the hut to which we had been taken. Then we asked to leave. Colonel Chavez flew away in his helicopter toward San Jose.

An hour later a reporter listening to a Costa Rican radio station heard the voice of Colonel Chavez come on the air. He announced he had found the North Americans. They were safe, he said, and on their boat. They had not been held hostage by contras. Their boat had developed engine trouble and the North Americans had gone into the jungle on the Nicaraguan side of the border for a picnic. That was why he could not find us in Costa Rica. For many days that lie became the official Costa Rican view of what had happened to us.

In the U.S. meanwhile, a reporter from Albany, New York, wrote a story for the *New York Post* while sitting in Albany. Fred Dicker's theory was that the Sandinistas had manufactured the kidnapping to make things look bad for the contras. I later saw a news interview of Fred someone had taped for me. While he had no evidence that the Sandinistas had been involved in our kidnapping — indeed, he had offered none in the *Post* story — his basis for believing it, as he said in the interview, was that our kidnapping "embarrassed Costa Rica by making it *appear* they can't control their borders. It makes it *seem* as if the Sandinistas care about peace and those against the government of Nicaragua don't." My experience confirmed both of those assumptions, but while I was still on the river, Fred Dicker filed a story — based on nothing — which lied about my experience.

When we returned to the U.S., people said we could have been dupes. How would I, who understood so little Spanish, have known whether those men in uniforms were Sandinistas or contras? It seemed obvious to me that a scam of that size would have had to fool more than just me. It would have had to fool the long-term Witness for Peace team who knew Spanish well and talked at great length to the men who said they were from ARDE. It would have had to fool the Nicaraguan boat crew who recognized Noel Boniche. It would have had to fool the villagers of El Castillo who worried about us while we were captured and welcomed us home when we were released.

Journal Entry, 8/9/85, El Castillo

The response last night was incredible. *"Queremos la Paz"* — We Want Peace — was being chanted from the dock for fifteen or twenty minutes while we were pulling in. It was dark and we were travelling with our flashlights again, moving very slowly toward the village lights. We got off the boat to TV cameras, crying women, staring children. It was just amazing. People kept hugging us and all the women were crying and the children wanted to touch us.

This morning we took a walk up to the castle on the hill which gives the village its name. The Spanish built it in the 1760s. It was first attacked by the British in 1840. We listened to the history of how many times this place had been attacked and I realized that last July they were living through a full-scale contra attack. Mortars, etc. with forty village people wounded, seven killed, sixty-seven contra dead. No wonder they could shout *"Queremos la Paz"* for that long.

Journal Entry, 8/10/85, San Carlos

Some of us have called home to relatives and lovers. They tell us what is appearing in the U.S. media. The press stories are so distorted. We are starting to make up our own. Peter and Kim decided what really happened was that we surrounded the contras and tortured them by singing *"Somos El Barco"* until they shot themselves.

I had planned to go to Costa Rica following the time in Nicaragua. I had never been to that country and thought it would make a nice vacation before I returned to the U.S. I knew someone in San Jose who was urging me to visit, and I had heard so much about the small Quaker community up in the rainforest, Monteverde, that I wanted to visit it. The only thing about my visit that wasn't changed by our capture was my itinerary. As soon as I returned to Managua, I called my San Jose friend. Yes, I should come, she said. Peace groups and churches and university groups wanted to hear what had happened to us. And so from August 17-25, 1985, I spoke to hundreds of Costa Ricans about the Rio San Juan.

Costa Ricans who value their democracy and unarmed neutrality needed to hear me say that I had been captured by Nicaraguan contras who appeared to operate freely out of Costa Rica and that I had been held on Costa Rican soil against my will for twenty-nine hours. Making that connection was so important for Witness for Peace that the doctor who had been with us on the boat, Ed Myers, a member of the long-term team, flew to San Jose to join me in the talks. On the second day a press conference had been scheduled for us. We went up to the legislative chambers where the event was scheduled. No one from the press came. One radio station was there. The newspapers had run Colonel Chavez's story and didn't need ours. We had to take out an expensive, full-page advertisement in *La Nacion,* the major Costa Rican daily newspaper, to tell our story. Finally one TV journalist taped an interview with us. He was Nelson Murillo Murillo, and he had his own reason for wanting to hear what we had to say: he had been badly wounded at La Penca in 1984 when Pastora had been holding a news conference and a bomb exploded.

But the Costa Rican people *did* want to hear our story and many of them came to our talks. They are intelligent people who have worked hard to maintain Costa Rica as the most stable country in Central America, and they have done it without a standing army since 1948. They know the Sandinistas are not solely responsible for all the border conflicts along the Rio San Juan. In *La Nacion* on July 28, 1985, they saw the photograph of fragments of a "Russian bomb" allegedly dropped from a Sandinista plane, fragments which clearly bore the English letters "TYPE BT" if you looked closely enough. They knew it was another staged event, another sample of the U.S.'s attempt to create a pretext for the invasion of Nicaragua.

Costa Ricans know firsthand that the U.S. and Japan and other nations that trade worldwide are frantic because the Panama Canal can no longer handle the traffic that needs to pass through it. They know that because a lot of the freight is being sent across Costa Rica in railroad container cars to deep water ports in the Atlantic and Pacific. And they know that physically the Rio San Juan is a natural canal, needing only about twelve miles of dredging to connect one ocean to the other. It is well reported in the Costa

Rican press that U.S. "farmers" have bought most of the land in northern Costa Rica along the Rio San Juan border, farmers and multinational corporations, that is. Nicaraguans and Costa Ricans know that the river itself belongs to Nicaragua, has been that country's by right of treaty for centuries. So owning the Costa Rican side of the river isn't enough. But the Nicaraguan government isn't selling. "We will build the canal when we can build the canal," they say, "and when we can support and defend it."

Following one presentation at the University of Costa Rica, a woman in the audience rose and asked me to take a message to "my" President Reagan. "Tell him to stop funding the contras," she said. "Tell him to stop these border incidents that are so dangerous to the peace and safety of our country. Tell him when we see the U.S. supporting such things, we can only believe that President Reagan wants a war in Central America, and he wants us to be the bodies."

After eight days of dealing with *the lie* in Costa Rica, I flew back to the United States, hoping things had been handled better here. After all, sixteen members of the international press corps had been with us on the boat. How could the truth of our kidnapping have gone unreported?

The truth had eventually been told, but when it follows a lie, it rarely has the same force as the original story. Five days after our release, the State Department admitted we had been captured by ARDE. It was in the fourteenth paragraph of an article which headlined the fact that one of the women in our delegation was sick (but she only had a cold, readers discovered in paragraph six). Most people have no idea that the State Department ever made a statement about who was responsible for capturing us and holding us hostage for those twenty-nine hours.

What happened to all of the film footage of us traipsing through the mud, I wondered. Friends with video, who had saved the news broadcasts, showed them to me. There we were, mud and all, but the stories accompanying the footage were incoherent. And then I remembered a story one of the Witness for Peace coordinators in Managua had told us the last day of our visit. A reporter for

Time news magazine had come into the office distraught. She had been sent a story by her New York office about our kidnapping. Revise it and return it, she was told. The story was so inaccurate, she said, it couldn't be revised, so she sent the thing back to them as it was and that was what ran. I remembered the journalist from NBC, then, who was assigning her video team to the boat with us; there was no soundtrack to accompany the film they sent back to New York. What I was seeing on the evening news broadcasts was a story written by someone in New York who knew no better than Fred Dicker what had happened to us. And they wrote the story to accompany some of the film footage, although by the time most of the film got back to the U.S. from the remote village of El Castillo, networks were no longer interested and newspapers had put us on the back page or dropped the story all together.

And so in the U.S. also, I told the story of the Rio San Juan over and over. This most recent telling — the writing and rewriting of this article — has spanned the vote by the Congress to send the contras another $100 million and the scandal of the Iran arms shipment payments being forwarded to the contras for arms which Congress had forbidden under the Boland amendment. During this time, I watched the one-year anniversary of the capture come and go. Late in the afternoon of August 7, 1986, I sat with a friend who had been on the boat, and we remembered being in the cocoa grove and talked about thinking we might be killed. And I remembered that moment of clarity — that I knew why I was there and that it was right for me to be doing this, no matter what else happened. If, in that moment of utmost extremity, some miracle could have transported me to another place to save my life, I would not have chosen it.

The morning after our release I walked along the river at El Castillo for a moment, looking for rocks. Rocks ground me, connect me to the earth; and I think I was looking for something concrete to remind me of what I had learned, of how I was feeling that morning. The rocks I was picking up were deep-rose quartz or marble, multifaceted, semitranslucent and shining with their own light and warmth. Several children soon joined me as I walked and took delight in my interest in these rocks that accompanied their everyday life. Then a woman about my own age with grey in her black hair came to walk with us. She was a teacher, she told me. She had taken her students further down the river in other years to study the unusual volcanic formations, but now the trip was too dangerous. I said I was a teacher, too, and I said how beautiful the rocks were, but I looked at the children as I spoke. Yes, she agreed, they were beautiful. Impulsively, she took a white flower she was wearing out of her hair and handed it to me. Then she gathered the children around her and they left for the school.

One of those rocks accompanied me as I travelled back to North America, to the United States, to Albany, New York. It sits on my desk and asks me to remember several things. It asks me to remember that Central America is not so far away or so foreign that I cannot understand what those people want for their own lives and the lives of their children. It asks me to remember that the suffering I saw in Central America is also here in the place where I live my everyday life. And it reminds me that the ability to share our privilege and to share our suffering is a gift, not a burden. That sharing is as fragile as a flower and as enduring as a rock.

Dangerous Memory

*...a people who want to live
looking forward.*

Villagers of El Castillo

Dangerous Memory

1.

My body knew the sound of a gun
before my brain. From the floor
of the boat where I had already
thrown myself, I thought,
that was a gunshot and was afraid.

Running this morning along the bank
of the Hudson I remembered

walking single file along the edge
of the Rio San Juan, not knowing
where I was being taken, strung out
along a jungle path as men
with guns told us where to walk
and how fast.
                I remembered the Hudson then,
remembered jogging one day with my dog
and how at the end of the run she had decided
she wasn't done running and slipped away
to play. As I searched along the riverbank
the sun was setting and dark was rising
from the dark river water. What I
had planned for myself — a run, then dinner
and a quiet evening — were no longer mine
to plan and the river seemed to whisper
give up, you can't control this now
as I searched and wept and cursed the dark
gathering along that riverbank.

And in the August heat, as a man
motioned me along with his rifle
I could hear the same whisper
you can't control this now
and felt myself grow numb as the sunlight
filtered through the jungle leaves
that whispered *surrender* in my ear.

I found my dog in pieces on the highway
later that night and wept and raged and mourned.
You loved her because of what she was
a friend reminded me. She loved to be free.
Her death was in
how she was in life
and if you loved her life
don't you have to love her death? I did
and wondered as I walked
through that jungle who would love
my death who would understand
what brought me down this jungle path.

2.

Later in Costa Rica I began to grow
separate from my body. I would talk
about coming close to death in the jungle
and wonder who had lived that experience
and find myself looking down at me
from a safe spot about six-feet overhead.
Oh, it must have happened to her,
I would realize as the voice that was mine
went on describing the mud and rifles
and the gentle face of the contra Israel
as he wrote a letter to his mother
balancing the pad of paper on his rifle.
Would he have shot you if the order
had been given? they asked. I didn't know
and faded further from myself.

In Costa Rica I talked about the Rio San Juan
and the kidnapping and how my tax dollars paid
these men to call themselves contras
instead of farmers. A man drove me up the mountain
to Monteverde to tell my story — green mountains:
a sanctuary for the birds and a preserve
to protect the endangered rainforest. As we
drove out of town he told me how sorry
he was he had given his name on the phone.
Stupid, that was stupid, he said as he checked
his rearview mirror. He was afraid
we would have an accident and wanted to hear
all the details: were the women in any
special danger? how did it feel to have a gun
pointed at me? and was I sorry I'd gone?
I shouted some answers over the grind
of the four-wheel-drive jeep as we wound
up the mountain, but when my voice broke
I stopped talking, afraid to begin crying.

That night I walked out of my room
into a noisy jungle. Below me on three sides
lightening flickered around the base of the mountain
and above the stars were sharp as cut glass,
bright as the glitter of a machete edge,
and totally unfamiliar.

One hundred and nineteen varieties of hummingbird
live in this preserve, irridescent turquoise and greens,
tiny thrums of wingbeat. I wanted
to go alone through the sanctuary
but there was someone to show me the trail,
point out the tree where the quetzals feed,
identify each endangered species. He walked
ahead on the trail, slicing with his machete
vines that threatened to block our way, and I followed
— unprotected — through the irridescent singing mist.

3.

Home once again, I walked out alone
nearly every day that first week. Or:
still floating just above my body,
I watched me walking out alone. The eighth day
I met my mother, dead eight years.
As she walked toward me I peered
into her face. She was crying and smiling
at the same time. I had questions
to ask her but we did not speak.

I wanted to know how I could go on
living with so much shame:

                    I mean
with the memory of the children sitting
at their desks in the school that was only
a roof. Those bright questioning eyes
welcomed me, tested the cut of my blouse
and hair, welcomed my foreignness. Last year
they huddled in ditches as mortars
shelled their village for twelve days.
Seven died. I helped buy the bullets.

                    I mean
with the memory of the old woman
who pinched my arm as I boarded the boat
to go down the river that had been closed
by war for thirty months, who pinched
my arm and pulled me back because she knew
what I had yet to learn. We came back
at night — freed because of who we were —
and when she found me and touched my arm
and cried *mi hija, mi hija,* I knew she spoke
of one who had not come back.

                    I mean
with the echo in my heart
queremos la paz queremos la paz
the cry of a people who want to live
looking forward, who want
life before death. After death
life takes care of itself.

4.

A year later I still walk
restless, pursued by questioning faces —
shrapnel-scarred children sit in my dreams
studying history books without words.
A contra named Israel writes a letter
with his rifle. The old woman has become
a singing child who dances by my side
reciting a brief joyful tale:
she sings it again and again until it
thrums in my ears like the hummingbird's wing —
sandino libertad ahora and the children
studying their empty books have grown old
waiting for the memory she spins to burn
through the mist.

Part of my memory is frozen
in that jungle. I see the red leaves of northeastern
autumn fade and shimmer into orchids hanging
from a rotted tree stump, languid as weeds
or the mottle of a parrot's crest. Nothing
that I look at will ever be again what it was
before.

At night I walk across a field as familiar as my own hand
lost in the questions I can't answer. I look back
at a light and for a moment become a woman
who is the last to leave a burning building,
gathering around her a few remnants
of a once-loved life, a backward glance
as the timbers begin to fold inward,
and then she steps toward the future.

The moon
rides high over my shoulder, bone-white,
telling no lies, crooning in the old woman's voice
this:

to stay sane when knowledge makes us mad
to believe in love even when it feels like death
to live as though the lives of others matter
to act when nothing is certain
to dream as if we could imagine a joyful tomorrow.

The Action Is The Prayer

> . . .we are all born into communities, whether we like
> it or not and whether or not we get along with the com-
> munity. And when I speak of 'doing one's first works
> over,' I am referring to the movement of the human soul,
> in crisis, which then is forced to reexamine the depths
> from which it comes in order to strike water from the
> rock of the inheritance.
>
> James Baldwin, *The Evidence of Things Not Seen*

Start with shame. That as an adult I have always been ashamed
of the spiritual community into which I was born, in which I was
raised. To be Christian, to be Protestant has seemed to me a
manifestation of the privileges that go along with being white, middle class, North American, privileges I have spent much of my
life attempting to come to terms with.

Did my religion ever mean anything to me? I was taken to Sunday school every week with my sisters. I learned the stories in the
bible, I suppose, but I know that my present knowledge of those
stories is not from those days, but from a course in comparative
religion I took in college and from my later interest in archetypes
and mythology. When I was twelve I was intensely involved in a
fundamentalist church for a summer, but I know now my interest
was in a thirteen-year-old cousin with whom I was infatuated. I
would have followed her anywhere and consider myself lucky she
only took me to bible study class.

Shame. I graduated from college in 1966 and went to spend the
summer with my family. They were stationed in Teheran, my father
a military officer somehow on loan to the Iranians even though
we weren't supposed to have a military presence there. I flew on
Pan Am flight #1 half way around the world with my younger sister. On the first Sunday in Teheran we went to church as a family,
as we always had when I was growing up. The minister was a mili-

tary chaplain, as he had always been. We sat in the pew in front of the American ambassador and his wife. There were the desultory songs, the offering, the sermon, and then the closing prayer. The chaplain called for "death and damnation to our enemies in Vietnam." I know he said it.

In 1961 I had gone to Antioch College wearing my U.S. Air Force sweatshirt, proud of what I thought it meant. But this was Iran in 1966. I had travelled in East Germany in 1965, and at every train station I had seen the signs sending "Greetings to our friends in North Vietnam in their struggle against the American aggressor." I didn't know where Vietnam was and had no idea how to respond when student friends asked me why the U.S. was invading Vietnam. That was also the summer of the Watts riots. Reading about the riots in the East German press, I distrusted the reporting. I knew they were exaggerating. Police in my country simply wouldn't fire on crowds. I told my East German friends confidently that they were being lied to by their press. Then a friend's mother sent him the clippings from his hometown Iowa newspaper. It was all true. And more. I began to wonder where Vietnam was.

I thought a lot about Vietnam and about the chaplain's prayer that summer in Teheran. I had to think about it, since refusing to go to church with my family required an explanation. What it meant to me, I realized, was that the religion I had been brought up in served the interests of my government before it served any spiritual need I might have experienced. And I thought then that if that was what prayer was — a petition to god to bring death and damnation to the enemies of my government — then prayer was an obscenity.

I have learned many things about prayer since that time. When my mother was dying and no longer able to talk with us, I sat with her in the hospital and remembered how when I was a child she had told me that she prayed every day. "I talk with god," she said. When I asked what that meant, she explained that when she walked down the street she told the grass how beautiful it was and thanked the flowers for being there and talked with the birds and squirrels.

It took a long time for me to understand what she was telling me: how she kept a "right relationship" with the world around her was through her daily prayer.

I called my friend Linda Hogan once and told her I didn't like the word *prayer,* that it embarrassed me. Didn't she find it embarrassing? There was a pause, then an exasperated, "Oh, you Christians!" I rushed to be offended, but she cut me off. "Judith, what do you think your poems are?" Of course. My poems are about creating a right relationship with my world, all parts of it. I imagine if I could have heard them, my mother's chats with the grass and the birds and squirrels might have sounded like poems.

When I decided to go to Nicaragua with Witness for Peace, the decision to make this trip with them was a difficult one for me. Witness for Peace is an organization which describes itself as an interfaith group committed to nonviolence whose objective is to change U.S. policy toward Central America. I prefer to think of myself as someone who believes in political solutions to problems; and while praying on the border between Honduras and Nicaragua has a certain dramatic symbolism, it was not clear to me how it was going to seriously challenge the reality of contra invasions and terrorist attacks on unarmed Nicaraguans. I was more convinced by the Nicaraguans' belief that when North Americans were present in their villages, the contras attacked less frequently, a reality they attributed to the contras' reluctance to kill citizens of the country providing their primary funding and support. When our delegation was asked to be an unarmed presence on the southern border, the Rio San Juan, the border between Nicaragua and Costa Rica, I was relieved. This was an action I could support unambivalently. We would travel a river that had been closed to civilian traffic for thirty months due to contra harassment, a river that was vital to the survival of peasant families farming along its banks. When we were fired on by U.S.-backed contras and captured and forced to march into the jungle on the Costa Rican side of the river, the political reality of our action became even more pointed. Costa Rica could not now claim that contra did not operate in and out of its territory.

When we were released and returned to the United States, I was surprised at how angry some people, many people, were at what we had done. Our local congressman said we had "holes in our heads" to have gone into a war zone and we deserved what we got. A caller on a radio talk show said no one would have been upset if we hadn't come back at all. Months later my sister said, "Well, you wouldn't call what you did religious, would you?" "Yes," I said, "I would." "No." She was quite firm. "That was a political action." And a woman in our delegation reported that a man at one of her talks wanted to know how much we had actually prayed on the trip. If we had prayed enough, the implication was, we could be called religious, but the minutes devoted to prayer had to equal more than the minutes devoted to political discussion. "I couldn't think how to answer him," she said, "and then of course in bed that night I knew what I wanted to say. I wanted to tell him that the action was the prayer."

The action was the prayer. I know that is true for me when the action is another way of creating a "right relationship" with my world. I had known it to be true when I was in college during the Civil Rights Movement and dozens of my classmates were "going South" for another kind of witness at lunch counters and on picket lines, on marches and in prison, a witness that carried serious consequences, even death, for some. And I knew it to be true in my first years as a college professor when news of Vietnam mobilized the college campuses and we went out on strike and faced the riot police's bludgeons and marched with candles the night the president said he would not run for office again.

My shame at Christian hypocrisy and apparent self-servingness began to be transformed into more complex feelings when I discovered liberation theology several years ago. Although I do not consider myself a Christian today, the realization that some North American Christians do indeed live in communities of resistance and solidarity with oppressed peoples made it possible for me to affiliate with Witness for Peace. And I am relieved that feminist theologians are helping all women who are members of patriarchal religions to struggle for their own liberation and to recognize their connections to other liberation movements. But for me, my most significant spiritual connection remains an action which helps me be in right relationship to my world.

I began this dialogue with my heritage by recognizing that I was raised in a religion, a faith, that was meant to be devoid of political content — unless that political content supported the status quo, the established power of the state, and remained implicit, not stated. That was the inheritance of my childhood. But the inheritance of my early adulthood was feminism, and in these recent years I have had to struggle also with the richness and limitations of that movement.

I believe it was that energy for transforming our world, that energy that comes from transforming our world, which so informed the early feminist movement and drew me — and many others — passionately into feminism. Most of the feminists I knew and worked with then certainly did not call the energy of our work spiritual, although the language of liberation theology could have described our experiences. We worked with love for change, change that enhanced the entire community. We sat in consciousness-raising groups and valued each woman's individual participation. We tried to understand that for feminism to become a radicalizing force in the world, white middle-class women would have to make issues of race and class central to our thinking, our discussions.

There were many successes and many failures, and both continue today. Even when our theory is grounded and remembers all the women we mean to include, we sometimes forget to connect our theory to our actions. Women's health-care systems, rape crisis centers, women's buildings and other projects have sometimes only been established by and for white middle-class women. Trained in the duality of the patriarchy, our words speak of our connections to one another; again and again our actions deny those connections. In liberation theology *sin* is the denial of solidarity. I think that denial has been the continual failing of the broad-based feminist movement in the U.S. The achievement of such solidarity, when it does occurs, carries a tremendous promise for the future of women and for our world.

To say the action is the prayer is one way for me to begin to make the essential reconnections. It requires that I make the changes in my life which will create my personal community as one of "right relationship" — with me and within the larger world. It is this work, finally, which I see as "doing one's first works over." None of us is responsible for being born into a particular community, but we are responsible for and to the communities in which we choose to live and love and work.

In recent years, I have found two communities that help me reconcile my ideas about change and my actions for change. The fellowship of recovering alcoholics is a profound connection and uses a program which recognizes that we are not alone in our struggles, that no life is a seamless cloth, but that each of us fails in our intentions at times and needs to heal, to mend, to make amends, to stitch our lives and the life of the common community back together. And the Albany Friends Meeting reminds me that the life of the spirit and the life of the world are not separate, that political work can be done in a manner that enhances the spirit. Without the understanding and support of these two groups, I could not have done the work I did in Nicaragua, could not today be working with Sanctuary, writing and speaking in ways that make me feel vulnerable. I have not abandoned those first all-important communities, of course. Blood family and the women in my feminist and lesbian families remain a bedrock, a continual support.

Standing by the Hudson River on a cold winter day, my friend said suddenly, "I wonder what it would be like to be the last ship coming down the river as the ice freezes behind it?" I know. I would be glancing over my shoulder to make sure I didn't get trapped in the past. I would be admiring the firm path of the wake frozen into the ice, showing where I had been. And I would be anxiously scanning the horizon for the next encounter.

Query

did you see
god today?

perhaps

in the shadow
of a gull
on a dune
when there was no bird

in the perfect
circle etched
on the sand
by a wind-blown weed.

I Ching

clouds move
on the silent
river mirror

leaf
and reflection of leaf
float rippled

as the sky
pulls moisture
back into the clouds

the separation
of heaven and earth
is a human fiction

I long to sink
like a rock
to the riverbed

or hover
molten raindrop
in a cloud

resisting
for this moment
the inevitable

downward pull.

Ilopango

for Karen Clark

Still
the stories

She went into the women's
prison in San Salvador
Ilopango   knowing
only the names
of two women who might
talk to her   it isn't safe
to talk to foreigners

my friend with her light
hair and green eyes
who told this story
could never be anything else

one of the women said
she had fought in battles
she was proud to be FMLN
wore her army green shirt
organized the women
in the political prisoners wing.

one of the women
had worked in a health clinic
was guilty   of vaccinating
peasant children
she wore a dress
nursed her infant daughter

Part of torture for every woman
my friend tells me   *still*
the stories
is rape   every woman
in that prison
had been raped many times
one of the women wore a dress
and nursed her infant daughter

the seed
of rape and torture
still this mother
the stories   decided
to love her child

and my friend had watched
the woman in the army green shirt
take the baby in her arms
cuddle the infant   laugh
and swing the baby high

she rules the hearts of all
the women here

still I hear
the stories

but this much love
I can barely imagine.

Sanctuary: A Journey

. . .the mesa became rock sculpture,
rising like proud elder spirits.

Road Leading to Big Mountain

124

Sanctuary: A Journey

The Sanctuary Movement, as it has come to be known, has no precise date of origin and no founders in the traditional sense. Early in 1980 the Salvadoran government imposed a State of Siege on that country which in effect marked the beginning of mass killings by the Salvadoran military. Human rights sources estimate that eighteen to twenty thousand people were killed or disappeared in that year alone. Thousands of Salvadorans fled the violence, fled northward across Mexico to the U.S. In the fall of 1981 the killings of hundreds of Indians in the Guatemalan highlands led to a similar exodus. The influx of refugees might have gone unnoticed for a while, since most fled at first to centers where other undocumented refugees lived. But in May of 1980 twenty-five Salvadorans who were crossing the brutally arid Sonoran desert were abandoned by their *coyote** guides. Half died and the incident made national headlines.

When the survivors were brought to Tucson and Phoenix, churches wanting to assist them discovered that the Immigration and Naturalization Service (INS) was planning to return the refugees to El Salvador, return them without informing them of their rights, without allowing any of them to file for asylum under the United Nations Protocol, which the U.S. had signed in 1967 and made the law of the land with the 1980 Refugee Act. That act provides for asylum if a refugee can demonstrate a "well-founded fear of persecution on account of race, religion, nationality, membership in a particular social group, or political opinion." The Tucson and Phoenix religious communities proceded to establish a task force on Central America to assist these and other refugees.

About a year later retired Quaker rancher Jim Corbett went to a local jail to help a young Salvadoran who was stopped by the Border Patrol and arrested. The Salvadoran had been shipped to another detention center, and every effort to find him and provide

---

*A man who smuggles refugees across the border for a fee.

bond for him during his appeal for asylum failed. Shortly there-
after — in an attempt to assist refugees before the INS could arrest and deport them — the "new underground railroad" began.
Corbett and others started harboring and transporting refugees
across the border. Within a year the need to house the refugees
within the U.S. became obvious. On March 24, 1982, six churches
in Arizona and California publicly declared themselves "sanctuaries" and began building communities of support for the growing number of refugees still seeking asylum. Churches and syna-
gogues all over the United States continued to declare sanctuary
and undertake the support of one or more refugees and their families. Two years after the first declaration of sanctuary, the Benedic-
tine Priory in Weston, Vermont, became the one-hundredth sanctuary congregation.

> *I don't think that is a day I will ever forget. . . Snow cov-
> ered everything and we were about a dozen cars of the
> new underground railroad, winding up the narrow road
> toward Weston Priory. As we came to the top of the hill,
> we could hear that all of the priory bells were ringing
> to welcome the Felipe Excot family of Guatemala into
> sanctuary.*

Roland Smith, Albany Friends Meeting

I first heard about the Sanctuary Movement in the summer of
1984. I was moving from my home in the country to a more con-
venient and affordable place in a nearby city. I didn't want to move
and was very focused on my sorrow at leaving the place that had
become home to me; no new place looks very promising in that
frame of mind. So I was both experiencing very real grief, and
also feeling sorry for myself, when a woman came into our week-
ly A.A. meeting, late and breathless. She said she had been volun-
teering as a monitor for some Central American refugees, a young
couple who had been in danger in their own country and fled, leav-

ing their child behind. She told us about the U.S. not granting refugee status to people fleeing El Salvador and that these particular refugees were in sanctuary at the Albany Friends Meeting House. Monitors were with them twenty-four hours a day to prevent the INS from arresting them without warning. If they were arrested and deported, she said, they were sure to be killed by death squads in their own country.

I knew there was a message for me in what she had told us. The next day I offered to be a monitor, and I met the two refugees from El Salvador. Hearing their stories, listening to their account of life so close to death — and not only death, but death by horrible torture and mutilation — changed my perspective on my own life. I began to read about Central America and the process these refugees were engaging in — the process of witnessing. It wasn't enough to be safe, the refugees were saying, they had to work for the people they had left behind who were not safe, and their work was to tell the story of what had happened to them for North Americans to hear and — hearing — to understand our role in the refugees' suffering. For it is our government, primarily, that is supporting the Central American military dictatorships with arms and assistance. The dream of these refugees, they told me, was not to become citizens of the U.S., but to return in safety to their own homes. We want El Salvador and Guatemala to be sanctuaries, they said.

I heard their stories. What does a white North American middle-class woman do with a story told by a man like Pedro Ramos? It was hard to imagine at first what context of my own life or experience I could bring to his account of the work he did on the Human Rights Commission in San Salvador. Each morning he would go out and photograph the new corpses left by the death squads — before their bodies were thrown in mass graves or on garbage heaps — so that there would be some record from which relatives could identify their dead. He carried with him negatives and some prints of those photographs, but I never asked to see them; the decapitated and mutilated corpses in my imagination were quite vivid enough. Later I saw the video Pedro helped make of the work

the Human Rights Commission was doing. In the video the direc-
tor of the Commission spoke against the death squads, and then
the video showed her funeral procession when she was assassinat-
ed not long after. Much later, when I was in Nicaragua, I met someone who had served on the Human Rights Commission with Pedro,
who had been there with him when the death squads bombed the
office. I had not doubted Pedro's witness, but hearing it in this new
context — when my own life was in danger — made me know its
truth in a different way. If he erred, it was in trying to protect us
from some of the brutal reality of his daily life in El Salvador.

Those of us who are feminists, who have lived the experience
of feminist process, know the power of witnessing. That was what
we did when we heard one another's stories of oppression or connection with the kind of attention that is nearly passion. We always knew the truth of a story, knew when the speaker had found
the core of what she was seeking to express. I know my life is not
the same today as it would have been if a feminist poet had not
stood in front of a group of academic women and challenged them
to hear their own hearts by exposing hers. My decision to live openly
as a lesbian in the moment I claimed that identity was only possible because I had met other women who were living openly lesbian lives.

Witness, I learned again in my life, is a circle. I heard Pedro
tell his story and my consciousness was changed by hearing him.
I decided to go to Nicaragua. When I returned I told my own story. If other lives are changed by the hearing, and others feel moved
to act differently, there will be new witnesses to that experience.
This circle is one of the primary reasons the women's movement
in the United States, indeed, in the world, is not dead, in spite
of the many obituaries prematurely written for it.

When I returned from Nicaragua, I understood that witnessing
is especially necessary when the reality of a lived experience is
denied by the culture at large, the culture to which the witness is
brought. That had not been as clear to me in a feminist context,
although to say it is to know it as true. Our experience as women
was denied or ignored in the patriarchal culture. Similarly, only

an infinitesimal percentage of the people who heard Pedro speak about El Salvador had any previous idea of where El Salvador is, and most would have denied that the U.S. is involved in a major air war there. After all, if it isn't on the evening news, can it be happening? When I came back from Nicaragua, news reports had so distorted the reality of what had happened to my delegation, that I was forced to witness what I had experienced.

who will be my witness?
. . .that same week I looked into the mirror
and nobody was there to testify;
how clear, an unemployed queer woman
makes no witness at all,
nobody at all was there for
those two questions: what does
she do, and who is she married to?

Judy Grahn, *A Woman Is Talking To Death*

Because this cycle of my life started with the Sanctuary Movement, I decided to go to Tucson during the trial of the Sanctuary workers to hear what kind of a case the government was making against their work, hear how they themselves would explain their work.

I began the trip to Tucson in New York City, in a sanctuary of another sort—the Dwelling Place, a shelter for homeless women near Times Square. Kathy, one of the women who had been in Nicaragua with me, lived and worked at the Dwelling Place and had invited me to visit. A week after she returned home from the Rio San Juan, Kathy woke up one morning and, looking out of her bedroom window, saw a woman lying on the steps of the church across the street from the shelter, a murdered woman lying in a pool of her own blood. She was a woman who had stayed at the shelter off and on, but the shelter has only eighteen beds and there are hundreds and hundreds of homeless women in that midtown area. There had been no bed for her that night, and she was murdered. I thought about the violence Pedro had described in El Salvador, remembered how prepared we were for violence in that war zone in Nicaragua, and realized more clearly than I ever had before how close to home the war zones really are if we choose to look.

Going to the Dwelling Place was not easy for me. I wanted to go and I was afraid to do it. What was I afraid of? I was afraid of being inadequate in the presence of other women's suffering. I was afraid of being a voyeur, of wanting to know, to see, so badly that I would intrude on the privacy of their lives. I was afraid I would be so different from them that I wouldn't be able to talk to them at all. I was afraid I would not be different from them.

When I finally got there, it was during the day when the shelter is closed to the women so that the staff can clean and prepare meals. I left at five-thirty, just before dinner, because I had an appointment. I was shocked at the mass of women waiting outside the door to get in. "What's for dinner?" several of them asked me. I said I didn't know, realizing I hadn't cared enough to ask. "But it smells great," I insisted. "You can't put a smell in your stomach," one woman reminded me as she stepped aside to let me out.

At breakfast the next morning, I ate with fifty or sixty women who were getting ready to go out on the streets for the day. It wasn't the worst possible day, even for December. The sun was out weakly and the temperature was only just below freezing. Some of the women sat with blank faces, others talked animatedly to one another. One woman sat at a table alone and talked. My friend introduced me to several women at the table where I was sitting and left. I talked first to an attractive younger Black woman who said she was a dancer. She could be, I realized, looking at her lithe body and her carefully fitted clothes. Carmen was job hunting, she told me, but it was hard when you went for an interview and they said, "We'll call you," and you don't have a phone. She had taken down the number of a phone booth and used it as her "home" phone, asking the prospective employer to call during certain hours when she would be there. Then she would go and stand by the phone booth, waiting for calls that never came. Sometimes she would call the employer back, but they get angry when you don't wait for them to call you, she told me. Carmen wasn't sleeping at the shelter, just eating breakfast and dinner there. She felt safer sleeping "out" — she gestured in the general direction of Times Square.

Another woman at the table had been listening to this conversation and wanted to talk. The daughter of Italian immigrants, Mary was living in a welfare hotel with her two children. By the time she feeds and clothes the children so that they can go to school, Mary doesn't have enough left to eat herself, so she comes to the Dwelling Place for a meal now and then. She has been in the welfare hotel for a year and a half while she searches for an apartment that will take her and two children for what welfare will allow — $260 per month. During that year and a half, welfare has been paying the hotel $2000 per month for Mary's single room and bath. That is nearly $40,000 wasted. To raise Mary's rent allowance $100 per month would be an infinitesimal dent in the city's welfare budget, even when she is multiplied by thousands of mothers in her position, compared to what is wasted on welfare hotels every year. Mary told me the City knows all of this. The City also knows the hotel showed a clear profit of $3 million last year. She read it in the *New York Times*. So did I.

At dinner that evening I sat next to Katrina who told me she was born in Zagreb (Yugoslavia) and that she was eighty-four years old. I couldn't imagine someone that age living on the streets and surviving for long, but she was very old and had clearly been living on the streets for many years. She spoke about moving to Seattle, about her sister and her son dying. There were no clear connections in her thought or conversation. It was impossible for me to know when these things might have happened or with what result. She ate her vanilla pudding while we were talking. Then she said she had indigestion, folded her paper plate of food into a neat bundle, and put it in her bag for later.

Later that night, when Katrina was back out on the streets spending an incredibly cold December night, I walked back up West 40th Street with my suitcase toward the subway entrance. Suddenly a very drunk, handsome Black man with long dreds swayed in front of me, peered into my face, and asked me, "What are *you* doing on 40th Street?" I had no answer. I looked back at him and shook my head silently, then walked on to the subway entrance. We don't call it *apartheid,* he is not an *untouchable,* but the lines are there, the stratifications are clearly drawn.

What does it mean to offer sanctuary to an individual who is on the other side of that line? Whether to a street woman in New York City or a refugee from Central America? People become refugees, in need of sanctuary, because of the lines that are drawn, lines of class, race, economics, ethnicity. It seems to me that those who draw the lines are those who also have the power to offer sanctuary.

I learned that in extreme situations when human lives and dignity are at stake, neutrality is a sin. It helps the killers, not the victims.

Eli Wiesel, April 19, 1985

I went to Tucson carrying my questions. I went with the assumption, I realize in retrospect, that the people on trial for aiding refugees must have had the same questions and must have answered them for themselves in order to do their work. While I allowed that the Sanctuary committee in my own town was made up of diverse individuals who held an incredible range of opinions and attitudes on everything from civil disobedience to abortion, I assumed that these eleven people had forged a more coherent rationale for their work.

I also went to Tucson under the illusion that I would be able to write something definitive about the Sanctuary Movement after this encounter. After all, I was an active member of my local Sanctuary Committee, I had read almost everything written about the political and religious implications of the movement, and I was writing a book myself about the concept of sanctuary. When I said I was writing about sanctuary, people nodded as though I still had my senses about me and asked how they could help. The Arizona Sanctuary Defense Fund Media office gave me a press packet that took me a week to digest. A Sister at the convent where I had been given a room offered me her entire file on Sanctuary: news clippings, articles, committee reports and minutes, her personal notes. I was overwhelmed. I went to bed the second night in Tucson realizing it would take me months to absorb the material I had already received. I wasn't sure I was the right person for this enormous project. The next morning I woke up remembering I was a poet, not an historian or journalist. I began to let myself sink into the atmosphere of the trial.

Each week of the trial began with a prayer service at seven-thirty in the morning where the defendants and some of their supporters gathered. I was surprised to walk into the Cathedral and find myself at a Quaker Meeting; the following week a rabbi conducted a short service. Each congregation connected to the Sanctuary Movement in Tucson participated in these services on a rotating basis. Feeling more at home, I introduced myself after the prayer service. Many people came up to me to ask after the refugees who had been in sanctuary in Albany. They had crossed the border at Nogales, south of Tucson, and were well known to some of the sanctuary workers there. During the interminable intercessions of the trial, people kept coming up to introduce themselves and others, to tell me who else was attending the trial, and to share information and support. Everyone I met knew about Witness for Peace, had heard about what happened to my delegation on the Rio San Juan, had done — in some way — support work to help get us released. I realized at the end of the first day of the trial that I felt myself a part of a national community, that I had a connection to these people and to what was happening at this trial.

I had decided to spend the entire day in court, taking only the breaks the defendants were allowed, so I could get a sense of what they were experiencing physically within the required structure of a courtroom day. The morning opened at 9:00 a.m. with Ellen Yaroshefsky, a defense attorney, cross-examining the primary witness for the prosecution, Jesus Cruz. Almost immediately her cross-examination was interrupted by prosecutor Reno's objection to her question. The judge called for a sidebar conference and Mr. Reno, all eleven defense lawyers and eleven defendants rose and went to the side of the judge's bench to confer on some point. Sometimes the defense lawyers would begin to argue rather loudly with the judge and the courtroom audience could get some sense of the issues. Then the judge would order the jury sent from the room, admonish the attorneys about their decorum, and the whole thing would begin again.

The first morning there were at least a dozen sidebar conferences, which made it very difficult to follow the argument the defense was developing against Jesus Cruz's allegations. Every question and answer, every piece of courtroom business, had to be translated, of course. Two of the defendants were Mexican citizens and Jesus Cruz himself spoke so little English that the defense had been able to call his credibility in doubt earlier in the trial when it became obvious that Cruz had no idea what was the content of the conversations he had so assiduously gathered with his tape recorder and body-bug. As the morning wore on with question, translation, objection, reworded question, translation, Cruz's response or request for clarification, translation, objection, sidebar conference — all I could think of was that getting at the information was like the slow drip, drip of water. And I wondered if water torture was like this: the anticipation, the wait, the event, then the long anticipation again. At the end of one day I was physically and emotionally exhausted.

After three days at the trial, I went down to Nogales, the border town where several of the defendants live and work. I wanted to see the holes in the fence which divides the two countries, holes which the Border Patrol could easily mend, but which are deliberately left in the fence in exactly the same places so that everyone will know where they are. At certain times of the year, I was told, the farmers need a lot of extra hands for harvest, and the undocumented aliens work for a fraction of the minimum wage for U.S. citizens. When the harvest is finished, the Border Patrol rounds up the workers, sends them back to Mexico, and the holes are guarded more closely. The government has never fined or arrested any farmer or rancher for hiring undocumented aliens, nor has the government ever objected to the ranchers sending vans and other transport down to the border to pick up the hands and take them to the ranches. Because of this, one of the countercharges of the Sanctuary defendants on trial in Tucson was "selective prosecution."

The contrast between the two towns, Nogales, Arizona, and Nogales, Mexico, was predictably depressing. I walked past the customs check on my way in and was assaulted by vendors looking for a quick sale. As the *peso* keeps being devalued, tourists flock across the border seeking bargains; these vendors were only trying to earn a living, I told myself, as I hurried through the tourist zone and into the heart of Nogales, Mexico. I had been given directions to the church where the prosecution said many of the refugees had been harbored and helped in their trip across the border. Nothing in particular distinguished it, just as nothing had distinguished the church on the other side of the border where refugees were received, or the motel where they waited for the drivers who would transport them on the first leg of this underground railroad to some relatively more secure place further north.

Alejandro Rodriguez is an El Salvadoran who was helped in this way. When the indictments were first handed down in January of 1984, Rodriguez was arrested out of the sanctuary church where he and his family had been living in Rochester, New York. During the cross-examination of Jesus Cruz, it became obvious how the government had known exactly where to find the Rodriguez family. Cruz befriended as many of the refugee families as he could, became their confidant and helper, gave gifts to the children, promised assistance with jobs and financial problems. Then he turned their addresses over to the INS. He was paid a sum of money for each arrest.

Alejandro Rodriguez was arrested and required to be a witness for the prosecution, required to give testimony against those who had helped him, those with whom he was in solidarity; if he did not give that testimony, he would be deported to El Salvador. Called to the witness stand by the prosecution, Rodriguez was immediately labelled a hostile witness by the judge. This meant that the prosecutor was allowed to ask him leading questions, an assumption of the witness's reluctance to give evidence having been made.

When he was asked if the person who had sheltered him in Nogales, Mexico, was in the courtroom, Mrs. Socorro Aguilar stood up proudly. She was crying. It was to become a familiar scene by the end of the trial, refugees asked to identify which defendant had helped, the defendants never denying they had given aid, for that was not the basis of their defense. Asked to give a simple identification, Mr. Rodriguez added his own testimony. He said of Mrs. Aguilar: "She was the only person that offered me a roof over my head when I was most in need. People told me she had a very good heart. I remember her with much love." Prosecutor Reno jumped to his feet, furious at this unsolicited information being presented to the jury, and objected. Judge Carroll upheld the objection and Mrs. Aguilar's heart was stricken from the record.

And so was every attempt to allow Mr. Rodriguez to explain to the jury why he had fled El Salvador, why he had been in need. The judge would allow "political persecution," but "torture" was not in the court's vocabulary; the witness could express "concern for his safety," but was not allowed to talk about death squads or murdered relatives. Finally the defense requested that Alejandro Rodriguez be allowed to tell his story for the record, but out of hearing of the jury. The court and the courtroom audience listened to the story of an El Salvadoran of some economic means, who owned a house and a farm, who was a labor organizer, who was arrested by the police without charges and tortured for fifteen days and then held for six months, who was released after a North American business associate "made inquiries" about him, who returned to his home in the dark of night to find a death squad camped out in front of it waiting for him, who fled to Mexico where he was later joined by his wife and children. As Rodriguez described seeing the death squad in front of his home after so many months away, a white-haired man sitting in front of me in the courtroom put his head in his hands and cried. The defense lawyers pleaded with Judge Carroll once again to let the jury hear this story; otherwise, they said, you rob him of his story and rob the jury of the chance to know the truth. "I have that discretion under the law," Carroll commented, as he denied the request.

On the same day at a sidebar conference, Judge Carroll told the defense lawyers: "I think people from Latin America perhaps have a difficulty in just answering the question 'yes' or 'no' by nature of their personal attitudes, maybe they don't." Appalled at the paternalism and racism in such a stance, the defendants asked the judge to disqualify himself, pointing out that the case primarily had to do with Latin Americans, depended on the testimony of Latin Americans, and that any prejudice of the judge could have an adverse effect on the trial. The judge seemed unconcerned about such an effect and also denied the right of one of the Mexican defendants to address the point, saying it would be inappropriate for a defendant to admonish the court. The same paternalistic attitude had earlier allowed Judge Carroll to deny the right of Native American plaintiffs against the forced relocation at Big Mountain to be heard in his court. Native people, he insisted, are not sophisticated enough to speak in his court and this "fact" was used to justify dismissing their suits.

It is obvious that the values of women differ very often from the values which have been made by the other sex.... Yet is is the masculine values that prevail.

Virginia Woolf, 1929

The paternalism in Tucson was not all on the side of the government. I spoke with a number of women who had been active in aiding the refugees. One had been a driver on the first lap of the underground railroad, going down to Nogales, Arizona, to pick up refugees who had succeeded in coming across the border. She drove them to Tucson or points north, drove them at considerable risk of being arrested by border patrols and having her car confiscated. There were several reasons this woman felt she could no longer work with the Sanctuary Movement. One was the way some of the men — white men with property, she emphasized — assumed the power of making decisions which affected the lives of many people without consulting those who were affected. Several of the women said that schedules had been changed, pick-up points rearranged, strangers (usually reporters) invited to go along on the runs, all without consulting the drivers. These women understood the necessities and uncertainties of such an undertaking, but did not understand why information could not have been shared with them when they were at risk. And several expressed concern that the refugees themselves were not consulted before being confronted by a U.S. reporter and/or photographer in this moment of extreme anxiety and stress.

Other women activists were angry that women had been doing much of the driving, most of the support work involving food, clothing and housing, and were getting little emotional support from the "hierarchy" and none of the credit. Certainly it is not the fault of male activists that the media has required heroes and has focused on one or two men it has declared founders of the Sanctuary Movement. Corbett is frequently cited as the first person to help El Salvadoran refugees: this is simply not true. I am sure that dozens of nameless U.S. citizens, many of them women, helped these fleeing refugees in any way they could in 1980 before Corbett happened to hear about the refugees' plight from a friend. Corbett himself has said, "Moses was the only founder of the Sanctuary Movement." Rev. John Fife's church was one of the first to declare Sanctuary in March 1982, but four others in California also declared sanctuary at the same time. I know that the process by which such decisions are reached is complex and difficult for a congregation, and I also know that women in these congregations are a moving force behind these discussions and the primary support when a refugee family moves into sanctuary. Neither Corbett or Fife, the media's touted founders, has talked about the major involvement of women in the Sanctuary Movement.

One of the women I talked with came to her activism in sanctuary through a political commitment to feminism and nonviolence.

She spoke of her concern — and sometimes her anger — when she perceived the Sanctuary Movement not wanting to be seen as acting from political motivation. She thought she heard some of the people who insisted they acted only out of religious conviction describing themselves as saviors of the Central Americans they helped across the border.

I believe the other side of that dynamic is that U.S. church people want the refugees to provide a "conversion" experience for the white U.S. church. In that sense the refugees become our saviors by allowing us to save them, to share their suffering from our place of comfort and safety. But both scenarios require the continued victimization of the refugees. It is a tradition frequent in the history of institutional Christianity, this insistence that "the poor will always be with us," an assertion that becomes a self-fulfilling prophecy. If Christianity needs the poor to minister to, then the poor had best not liberate themselves. The refugees themselves have a very clear analysis: they want El Salvador and Guatemala to be sanctuaries in which they can live, and they believe that for us to help means that we are helping them to achieve that goal, the political goal of liberation and self-determination, not perpetual victimization. Some of the sanctuary defendants and other sanctuary workers support that analysis wholeheartedly.

I had also expected to find that the sanctuary defendants had a clearly articulated consensus about civil disobedience, another misconception I quickly put aside. Some told me they had intentionally committed civil disobedience by aiding the refugees. Some said they had not broken the law; it was the INS that was breaking the law by not granting refugee status. Sister Darlene Nicgorski pointed out that as long as sanctuary workers had aided refugees silently — that is, without making political connections about why the refugees had to flee their countries — the U.S. government was perfectly happy to have bandaids applied to this trauma. It was when some sanctuary workers began to network with political Central America support groups that the investigation began, the infiltration of churches, the arrest of North Americans who were giving aid.

Not one of the sanctuary workers with whom I talked ever doubted that it was right and moral and ethical to help the refugees. I read editorials in the local newspapers questioning what it meant that religious people were on trial, particularly those who were officials of the church. Didn't such people have a special obligation to obey the law, the editorials asked. What kind of example are they setting for our young people? This concern expresses a conflict Carol Gilligan* describes as one between a "morality of rights," which is based on an assumption of equality, and an "ethic of responsibility," which recognizes differences in need. It is the former which argues for the denial of immigration status to Central American refugees because native U.S. workers have a right to available jobs. The latter sees individuals without food or shelter, and works to provide them. The "morality of rights," it seems to me, is also predicated on an assumption of limited resources to which certain people have an innate right, and while an "ethic of responsibility" does not necessarily assume unlimited resources, it does require that they be shared first with those most in need.

> *We are created sojourners in a land we did not make, a land with no meaning of itself and no meaning we can make for it alone. Who are we to demand explanations of God?*
>
> Annie Dillard, *Holy The Firm*

Several times during the month I was in Tucson I went alone out to the desert. I especially loved the desert at night — the vast silence which matched the vast starry sky, the abrupt interruption of the coyotes playing along the edges of consciousness. I climbed Mount Ajo down in Organ Pipe Cactus National Monument, the furthest southwest corner of Arizona. At the top of the mountain I sat in the sun that was hot even in January and looked out over California to the west, Mexico to the south. For miles and miles

---

*Carol Gilligan, *In A Different Voice* (Harvard University Press, 1982).

there was desert scattered with a few sparse cactus, the occasional greenish line of an arroyo winding through the pale brown sand. I wondered what it must have been like to be one of the women or children fleeing El Salvador who were abandoned in this stretch of desert in 1980. I remembered seeing a picture of one of the women who survived, her large dark eyes lined with tragedy. Then, I had never heard of the Sumpul River massacre in which 600 women, children, and elderly people were killed by the combined units of Honduran and Salvadoran militaries as they tried to flee toward safety, away from the bombs and white phosphorus wiping out their villages and homes, liberating them from the "communist insurgency." That happened in March. I wondered if any of the refugees abandoned in the desert a few months later had been trying to cross the Sumpul River that day.

As I sat on the mountain top, a hawk winged across the canyon beneath me, looking like it belonged to the earth instead of the sky. The saguaro cactus here have a kind of majesty like the giant redwoods — not so large, but massive for what they are — that feeling of endurance, of age, and even wisdom. When they start to die, their arms droop. It is another world. And yet the eyes of the woman abandoned in the desert seemed to me very like the eyes of some of the women with whom I had eaten in the shelter near Times Square only a few weeks before.

While I was in Tucson I gave several talks about the Witness for Peace trip on the Rio San Juan. I had been giving these talks since the day I left Managua, first in Costa Rica and then in the U.S. I spoke to Central American activists, to religious groups, to women's groups, to university students, and others, ranging from the most sophisticated and aware audiences to listeners who had to be shown where Central America was on a map and told a brief history of U.S. involvement there before the capture of our delegation by contras could make any sense to them at all. When I began giving the talks in the U.S., I was immediately able to say to those like my congressman — who felt we were crazy to have left home and gone to a war zone and so deserved what we got — that Nicaraguans don't have to leave home to be in a war zone, a war zone created in part by congressmen like New York's Stratton and Solomon and D'Amato who voted funds for the violent overthrow of an elected government. In Nicaragua I met children who had been scarred by shrapnel from bombs and mortars manufactured in the U.S. and carried to them by U.S. mercenaries like Eugene Hasenfus. He, of course, did not deserve what he got for going into a war zone. He is an American hero.

As the immediate shock and trauma of the capture began to recede for me, I began to experience other emotional connections which helped me understand that event in a broader context. The first time that happened was when I heard Kathy tell about waking up and seeing the murdered woman from her bedroom window in New York City. That homeless woman, I realized, also did not have to leave home to be in a war zone. It was then I decided I needed to visit Kathy at the Dwelling Place, and it was then I began to ask audiences, who were mostly white and middle class, to consider — as they worked to help Central American refugees — how many people were at risk here in the United States: Black people, Indian people, working-class and unemployed poor people, gay and lesbian people. I asked them to make the connection back to a political and economic system which puts all of these people at risk and had made refugees of so many Central Americans.

In November I was asked to speak at a memorial service for the four churchwomen killed in El Salvador. In preparation I was given some material written by one of the women, Sister Ita Ford. I was particularly moved by a quotation from a letter she had sent home to those who were worried about her safety in El Salvador. "You say you don't want anything to happen to me," she wrote. "I'd prefer it that way myself — but I don't see that we have control over the forces of madness, and if you choose to enter into other people's suffering, or love others, you at least have to consent in some way to the possible consequences."

I began to think about what she was suggesting — that love itself was a risk and when we choose to love we open ourselves to the consequences of that loving. I was beginning to understand that I didn't have to go to Nicaragua to be at risk, although sharing that risk was an expression of love. Nor did I have to be a homeless woman living on the street; I had only to open my eyes and my heart to a new seeing, a seeing that would allow I had some relationship to her, some responsibility to her, a responsibility that would then require me to act, to move toward creating change, toward creating sanctuary.

We all need sanctuary, that is clear to me. We all need a safe place in which we can love and learn and grow and do our work. Sometimes we call this safe place home. Sometimes we call it family. What I was experiencing when I wrote the ending of the poem "Leaving Home" was a loss of that safe place, a loss that I experienced as being cut loose from roots, from familiar things, separated from someone and someplace I loved. That home was all of those things for me, and yet it was not those things. I was a feminist working among people who did not share my values, my understanding about what a woman could be and do in the world. I was a lesbian living in rural, conservative, Christian America. I lived on a dirt road in such isolation that on some nights my lover and I slept with the baseball bat and chopping maul next to our bed. Those were nights when we received harassing phone calls, or when cars roared past the front of the house honking, or when our mailbox was blown up by someone dropping an explosive in it. That sanctuary was not an illusion, but it was certainly an artificial construct, one I created by ignoring — when I could — the differences and the danger in the world around me. I would suggest that — barring a leap into utopia — all sanctuaries share this characteristic. We construct them as best we can, shore them up against the real and perceived and imaginary dangers in our environment, defend them and try to preserve them.

What does it mean, after all, to offer sanctuary to refugees from El Salvador or Guatemala. Does it mean we can protect them from the INS if that agency decides it really wants to arrest them? Probably not. Does it mean we can keep them from being deported back to their countries of origin if they are arrested? It is doubtful. What does it mean, then, and what is it worth? The Sanctuary Committee in Rochester had to answer that question when Alejandro

Rodriguez was arrested. He was accused of being a communist sympathizer because he had visited Cuba once in the 1960s. He was rearrested in May, and because of his high risk status (that is, he was perceived as posing a great threat to the U.S.), his bail was set at fifty thousand dollars. The Sanctuary Committee raised that bail in a few hours on a Memorial Day weekend when the banks were closed and brought him home to sanctuary once again. But neither Rodriguez or the committee thought there was any chance now that his application for asylum would be granted by the U.S. He knew if he was picked up again he would be deported. And so one night during the summer, Alejandro and his family fled. They were forced to flee at night and in secret, just as they had been forced to flee El Salvador. For the Rodriquez family sanctuary meant a loving and concerned community of U.S. citizens who agreed he would be safer somewhere else, who helped him get to that place, who were willing to accept the loss of fifty thousand dollars rather than the loss of their friends.

For other Sanctuary Communities, accepting refugees into their homes, opening their families to these people who are in need, has exposed them to real difference, close-up, for the first time. To offer sanctuary has meant to confront racism and religious bigotry as it affects someone who lives with them and for whom they are responsible, to confront that racism and bigotry in their neighbors, their own families, and themselves. To offer sanctuary has also meant looking face to face at suffering beyond what most white middle-class North Americans have ever known. We tell the state to build shelters for the homeless. We let social service agencies deal with the battered and brutalized women and children in our midst. But seldom has there been an occasion on which this suffering has been voluntarily brought into our homes. And by suffering beyond the ordinary I mean, of course, beyond the pain we have encountered, some of us more than others, of incurable illness, of accidents, of failures, of addictions, of children lost prematurely. I mean the suffering of torture and mutilations inflicted without reason or explanation. We understand the answers when we ask members of our own communities, how were you hurt? why were you hurt? But few of us who are white, North American, and born into a Christian majority, have a context in which to understand the answers we receive when we ask that question of refugees fleeing El Salvador and Guatemala.

Jews and Jewish communities involved in the Sanctuary Movement have, of course, a different history of suffering and bring to their commitment an experience that enhances the understanding of sanctuary for all of us. Rabbi Gerold Serotta, a founder of New Jewish Agenda, insists that Jews, "especially because of our history, should be involved in sanctuary. When there are people fleeing oppression and danger, the Jewish community of all communities should be involved." Joseph Weizenbaum, who is rabbi of the Sanctuary Congregation Temple Emanu-El of Tucson, agrees that "the true response to the Holocaust is to do everything possible to see that nowhere in the world should such murder reoccur." Like many Jews, Weizenbaum's experience of sanctuary is more immediate, personal, and painful than many white Christians. His father, he says, was an undocumented alien who came into the U.S. as a stowaway on a ship in 1913. Two relatives living in Europe in 1942 "sought sanctuary in their community and were denied. They are now numbered among the six million." To do nothing when confronted with the need of these refugees from El Salvador and Guatemala, says Weizenbaum, is to imitate the "innocent" Germans who did not murder the helpless, but insured their deaths by failing to stop the murders.

The conscious connection the Sanctuary Movement has made to the original Underground Railroad is an important one. It is an effort to say we must try to stop the murder of the helpless, no matter what their legal status. It was against the law of the land to aid runaway slaves, just as the government now claims it is illegal to help these Central American refugees. People who provided assistance to Blacks fleeing the South said they were following a higher law, as many do now. Most of the people fleeing El Salvador and Guatemala are people of color. Many have been part of a virtual slave population, a status that is ensured by an economic system in which — as in El Salvador — fourteen families own about 90 percent of the land. Coming north does not mean coming north to freedom, just as it did not mean that to the slaves fleeing the Confederacy. It means coming to a place where issues of survival are somewhat less immediate, but where a refugee without documents is still subject to work at substandard wage, when work can be found at all; it means coming to a place where a refugee can be picked up and detained in prison and then deported; it means coming to a place where racism may kill or maim the refugee even if some government docs not.

Most white North Americans don't like to be reminded of this view of our country. We prefer to think of the legends of generosity and selflessness which co-exist with the reality of the Ku Klux Klan, lynching, and mob actions against Black citizens, not only in the distant past, or the near past, but today. Where was the underground railroad in Queens, I wondered, when a gang of white men attacked three Black men outside a pizza parlor? When a mob of white residents tried to force a Black couple and an interracial couple out of their homes in a predominantly white section of southwest Philadelphia? When Black women and children tried to flee their burning home in the Move massacre of 1985 and were met with bullets and finally a bomb? And what is my responsibility?

Basta, says the Sanctuary Movement. *Stop.* Stop the killing. Stop the suffering. It is enough. And in saying *basta,* we are changed. It is a process, says refugee Pedro Ramos, which begins when a sanctuary worker first helps a refugee, reaches out in a humane way to someone in need, and does not stop there, but continues to learn, to understand the root of the refugee's suffering. And this understanding requires more concrete steps, more specific ways of saying *basta.* To deny the process, to deny the political, the profoundly political implications of the process, is to short-circuit the work of sanctuary. It is to become like the "innocent" German who did not kill and who did not stop the murders. When we accept the process, accept the label of *political,* if that is necessary, I believe we go through a door that only opens one way and leads to an infinite number of other doors inviting us into new possibilities.

Sister Darlene Nicgorski calls the process *acompanamiento,*
solidarity, to accompany. "One begins down a path; little choices;
go to Guatemala, help start a preschool and there is no turning
back. The road grows narrower and more lonely while our eyes
see more clearly the causes and roots of oppression." When the
INS searched her house and confiscated an article Nicgorski had
written, they circled the expression "option for the poor," which
she used, and in the margin they wrote "Marxist Ideology." If it
had not been clear to her before, it certainly was obvious in that
interaction that "siding with the poor, accompanying them in their
struggle, in their exiled state is a political act."

I have been thinking, too, of the thirteen-year-old white boy in
Philadelphia who chose to testify as a lone witness against his white
neighbor who had spray-painted the words, *We Don't Want No Nig-
gers KKK,* on the front of a house which a Black family had been
considering buying in a white neighborhood. "You ruined my
brother's life," the man's sister accused the boy. "What about his
children?" she asked. "What about the children of Mrs. Denson?"
the boy retorted, referring to the Black woman who had wanted
to buy the house.

That boy will be a different man than he would have been if he
had let the moment pass. It was a choice, a little choice, to be a
witness, but he has gone through a door which only opens one
way. Someone at his school put a picture of him on a pole labelled
Rat, but he says he has no regrets. He has given up a little of his
safety, the safety of anonymity; there is no way to measure what
he might have gained.

I think I begin to understand what Ita Ford meant when she
referred to the possible consequences of loving others. For sanctuary is about crossing lines, about creating connections rather than
exclusions. If I choose to create my own safe place by closing my
eyes and my heart, then I will not be safe for long.

It is ironic. Sanctuary is about living dangerously. Sanctuary is
about taking risks beyond the ordinary. Risks of class security or
race security. Risks of the heart. Physical risks. I have never in
my life felt as secure in myself as during those twenty-nine hours

of captivity on the Rio San Juan. I knew well I might be killed. But I also knew more clearly than I had ever known before that I was in the right place. I was in the right place in that jungle and I was in the right place in myself. Taking the risk allowed me to be the person I had always wanted to be. What I have had to learn since I have been back in the United States is that I do not have to travel to take that risk, to be that person.

Give Me Liberty

It's Liberty Weekend
at the shelter for homeless
women   just off Times Square
behind the bus station
in the zone they call
hell's kitchen
the women are gathering
in the lounge so as not
to miss a minute of the fun.

There she is
the lady with the torch
corporately crafted image
of freedom   they call it
liberty and mean by that
the liberty of free
enterprise: you want to put
that lady with the torch on your
bluejeans
soda pop
hamburgers
silver coins
silver coins
silver coins?
No problem. The appropriate fee
will guarantee your corporate
image will be untarnished.

And now the ladies
in front of the tv
rise en masse
oh say can you see
the harbor from here?
It's only forty blocks
from Times Square to the Battery
forty blocks and a lifetime
forty blocks and the price of a ticket
a year or two or three's income
for these women, so
say can you see enough
on the black and white tv in the lounge
ladies, it's all they've got for you.

There's a shot of the harbor
with the tall ships
sails furled or sails lofted
graceful majesty in every line.
Now that's real pretty
every head in the lounge nods
agreement as the tv camera
pans up the line to the lead
ship   *The Esmeralda*
so pretty it could break
your heart   or your body
but here in America we don't hold
a ship's past against it
after all no one was tortured
there today or even yesterday
today the broken bodies
sit in this lounge or rest in a doorway
each past unforgiven.

And now the fireworks
it's a burst of glory
a long drawn sigh
oooooooohhhh
and then the climax
symphonies and marching bands
another burst of light
oh, it's too bad you don't have color tv
here in the lounge of the shelter
give me your tired
the announcer intones
and the women stand up with a single
impulse   your poor your homeless
give me your five thousand
dollars for a seat at the feet
of lady liberty and you'll get
the fireworks in technicolor   oh, yes.

That's it for tonight
and the ladies gather
their bags   some head for the exit
some sit waiting to be told
they must leave
give me your poor
for there are only eighteen beds here
your tired and hungry and lonely
the other seventy or eighty women
who are here tonight in the lounge
give me your homeless
will dwell in the shadow
of hell's kitchen tonight.

Looking For Home:
The INS v. Margaret Randall

She walked slowly up the canyon path behind her house in Albuquerque, New Mexico, and waved her hand toward the harsh, brown mountain. "This is where I want to do my work," she told me. Not an outrageous wish for a woman who grew up in this landscape, one might think. But in 1967 Margaret Randall gave up her United States citizenship to become a resident of Mexico, and last year the U.S. Immigration and Naturalization Service (INS) denied Margaret Randall's petition to reside again permanently in the country of her birth.

Author of nineteen books of poetry, nine books of prose and oral history, dozens of essays and translations, Margaret Randall, says the INS, goes "far beyond mere dissent, disagreement with or criticism of the United States and its policies" in her writing, and for that reason she will be excluded from this country in spite of being a former U.S. citizen, being married to a U.S. citizen, being the daughter of U.S. citizens, and being the mother of children who are U.S. citizens.

Who is this woman? She is the forty-nine-year-old mother of four grown children; she is a poet and photographer and teacher. She is the subject of a lawsuit brought *against* the INS by a group of well-known authors who allege that their constitutionally protected right to associate with and receive information from Randall is being violated by her deportation order. What has she done to be the subject of these varied concerns?

Born in New York City, Randall moved to New Mexico with her parents when she was ten. She lived in New York City again as a young woman, a single parent raising a child. She moved to Mexico in the late 1960s for economic reasons, she said, and it was also for economic reasons that she relinquished her U.S. citizenship. She says at that time it was very difficult for an alien to get any employment in Mexico.

She later married a Mexican citizen, poet Sergio Mondragon. With Mondragon she began the bilingual literary magazine, *El Corno Emplumado,* which published writers like Denise Levertov, Thomas Merton, Octavio Paz, Ernesto Cardenal, and Allen Ginsberg. The magazine took a strong stand against the Mexican government's repression of the student movements of the sixties, and when the government closed down all of the literary magazines in opposition to its policies, *El Corno Emplumado* was able to continue with the help of financial backing by U.S. citizens. That infuriated the Mexican authorities, Randall remembers, and one day two men came into her house and at gun point took her papers. It was 1969. She was terrified. "We had to go underground. At that time I had four children. The youngest was three months old. I had to leave. I sent my children first."

She fled to Cuba where she lived for ten years, writing and publishing such books as *Cuban Women Now,* stories and interviews with Cuban women who describe their lives in modern Cuba. She also travelled to Vietnam and Peru at the invitation of the United Nations to write about women.

In 1979 Ernesto Cardenal invited Randall to come to Nicaragua to document the lives of Nicaraguan women before and after the Sandinista revolution. Again, her books were oral history documents which gave a voice to previously voiceless people. *Sandino's Daughters* and *Christians in the Nicaraguan Revolution* are essential reading for anyone who wants to understand Nicaragua today. In 1984 Margaret Randall came home to Albuquerque.

"How can writing go beyond mere dissent?" I asked her. "Did you ever advocate the violent overthrow of the U.S. government?" "No," she insisted, half laughing, yet looking troubled. "They don't even claim that. They don't claim I was a member of the communist party. I never have been. They don't accuse me of any of the other thirty-three deportable offenses on their list. They accuse me of having called the police 'pigs' in a poem of mine in 1972. They accuse me of having called the Attica prisoners 'my brothers' in a poem in 1972. They accuse me of spelling America with three K's in the Sixties. People ask me, 'Do you really think it's just because of your writing?' The INS makes that abundantly clear. It's purely what I've written, and of course the fact that I've written enthusiastically about countries like Cuba and Nicaragua."

At issue here, according to the writers who have brought the suit against INS asking that Randall be allowed to stay, are constitutional rights. The First Amendment does not permit the government to exclude someone from this country simply because that person's views are not consistent with the views of the administration in power. Margaret Randall never built or planted a bomb; she never advocated that others should. She was critical of U.S. foreign policy in Vietnam and said so forthrightly. As an editorial in the *Albuquerque Journal* concluded, "Randall's trade is in ideas and philosophies. And that, rather than a perceived threat to the United States, is what this debate is about."

What will it mean for her personally, I asked, if she is not allowed to stay in New Mexico? "Not death or torture, as it has meant for so many others," she is quick to acknowledge. "It means I will have to go someplace else."

We talked about sanctuary, about finding a safe place in which she could work and grow, a place she could call home. Did she find that kind of safety in Cuba, I wondered. "Yes, we did find that kind of security in Cuba. One of my children, as a matter of fact, opted to stay in Cuba. And I think that kind of security exists in Nicaragua, and I'm sure that it exists in the liberated zones of El Salvador, although I've never been to them. There are pockets of that kind of security all over the world where people have gotten together and are building something which is true to their own concept of what their needs are and not so much based on the media hype of what we are *taught* our needs are in any of these countries. The problem, I think, arises for me and for many people in that one does have a place and that place often is not Cuba or Nicaragua or the liberated zones of El Salvador. My place is in New Mexico."

When we had been walking in the canyon behind her home earlier in the day, Randall gave me a glimpse of what "having a place" might mean to her. As a child she used to tell her parents she was spending the night with a friend. "I would go off with geological survey maps and sleep out in the desert. I would follow a map until I couldn't see telephone wires or electrical posts. I would walk until I was in a place where there was nothing that spoke of the twentieth century. Then I would imagine I was living on this land before the Spanish conquest. I would imagine that situation until I fell asleep. I did this dozens of times as a young woman in New Mexico."

Margaret Randall says that she is by nature an optimist. I said that I sometimes despair because we aren't making the progress I think we should be making, because we aren't making progress that is measurable. Even though I know I should be able to remember that the process of building and changing is more important than measurable progress, still I despair. "I really don't," Randall insisted. "When I look at the magnitude of the machinery they have going against us, I wonder how we've done as much as we've done." Her idea about sanctuary, Margaret Randall says, is that we are creating a safe place, but in little bits and pieces. She referred to the risk that Harriet Tubman took in the Underground Railroad to bring slaves north to a country that was only slightly less racist than that which they had left. Sanctuary, she was saying, is a margin, sometimes a very narrow margin. Her case is part of that building, part of the work of sanctuary.

"We're building a world where women can be safe or Blacks can be safe, where Chicanos can be safe, where Native Americans can be safe, where gays can be safe, and disabled people and children and men and all people," insists Randall.

At the Deportation Hearing held in March of 1986, INS prosecuters had apparently a very different understanding of the world they want built here in the U.S.

> *Gonzalez:* You worked at various jobs in New York, some of which included being a waitress in a gay bar, correct?
> *Randall:* That's correct.
> *Gonzalez:* Okay. Among the other jobs that you held at the time were as a nude model, right?

Randall: Are you going to talk about the jobs I had or
  are you just going to pick out. . .
Gonzalez: I'm asking the questions. I'd like you to try and
  answer that question. Were you working as a nude
  model?
Randall: Yes, I worked as an artist model.
Gonzalez: In the nude?
Randall: In the nude and not in the nude.

The implication in the government's line of questioning is that
it is illegal, or at least a deportable crime, to work in a gay bar
or to pose as an artist's model. Margaret Randall was out of the
country during most ot the rebirth of feminism here in the U.S.
in the late sixties and seventies when feminists fought against
stereotyping women by their sexual preference, by their survival
choices of work. She was in other countries writing about wom-
en's work and lives in cultures where women's survival issues
seemed different, more immediate. Now, back in the U.S., she is
herself faced with issues of survival, not life-survival probably,
but the next level: where can she live, work, love? Her choices
in these areas have made her an outlaw in the country of her birth,
an outlaw in company with her sisters who have chosen to live
as lesbians, as single parents, as women-in-community on the land
in rural areas and in collectives in urban settings, or in any non-
patriarchal structure.

On September 2 the judge who heard this case upheld the INS
ruling that Margaret Randall should be deported. He based his decision on her writings. His ruling confirmed that it is a deportable
crime to criticize the U.S. government in print, even if history proves
the criticism to be well-founded. And women know there is another
message in this decision, a message which tells us to obey, to accept authority, to accept those patriarchal limitations on our life
choices. The ruling will be appealed, but it will be a long uphill
battle — a journey that will probably require all of Margaret Randall's stamina and optimism.

Travelling Through Big Mountain

I sat on the dirt floor of Katherine Smith's hogan as she pre-pared fry bread over an open fire. Outside, only a few hundred yards away, run the high-power electrical wires that carry electricity down to Phoenix and Los Angeles, but in this hogan there is no electricity, no phone, no running water.

I had come to the Navajo/Hopi reservation to meet this woman and to see for myself the landscape of Big Mountain. I had been told this area is sacred to the Hopi and Navajo peoples, and when I left Katherine Smith later that night and drove the many miles of dirt road leading to a highway, I understood that belief in a new way. The moon was full; it highlighted the mesa rising, first on one side of the road, then on the other. At one bend in the road the mesa became rock sculptures, rising like proud elder spirits shimmering in the moonlight.

I had come to this hogan to say thank you to Katherine Smith for her endurance and her vision. I only meant to stay a few minutes, for I did not want to intrude, but her youngest daughter, Mary, told me that I could not leave a Navajo home without eating or it would be a great shame to them. "If we have sixty visitors a day," she said, "we eat sixty times." So I settled back onto the dirt floor and watched as she mixed the flour and a little of the precious water, opened a can of beans and placed it on the fire to warm.

I told Katherine Smith that I was a writer, and she said that she had written something once on a flag. What she wrote in the white stripes on the flag was that it had become the flag of cheaters and liars and greedy people who only wanted money. She wondered if U.S. citizens ever remembered what their flag had originally meant.

When the fry bread and coffee were ready, we all ate: first the company, then some of the family, finally Katherine herself. Her oldest son, Julian Begay, who was visiting, told me I should try a piece of the corn bread that was with the fry bread in the pan we were eating from. He said it was baked in an in-ground oven for a puberty celebration; when a young girl becomes a woman, Navajos bake this special kind of bread. I tasted it. At first it had a kind of fragrance, but by the second or third bite it was like corn bread, only a little grainy and very dry. He said they also used to have a ceremony with this kind of bread on the day when a baby in the family laughed for the first time, and I thought that was wonderful, to have a celebration when a baby laughs and becomes part of the family.

After we had eaten, Katherine began to talk a little bit about the day she had first seen the men building the fence across her land. She was out with the sheep. She said, "I was alone and I saw them and went over to them and told them to stop, that they weren't to build a fence there. They went away that day and the second day they came back and were building the fence again and I went in and got that old rifle," she gestured toward the corner where an old single shot rifle stood, "and went out. There was a Hopi man dropping fence poles into the holes from a tank. They were using an old tank with a white star on its side to build this fence, a tank like they had used in Vietnam. And I thought that if they were going to make war in their own country, then I would respond. So I fired a shot over the head of the Hopi man who was dropping those fence poles into the holes and he just flew to the ground. He absolutely fell off the tank. Then I walked over to the policeman by myself and three policemen arrested me and took the gun and took me to Chinle to prison."

At that point Julian began to tell the rest of the story. Chinle is on the other side of the reservation, about sixty miles from Big Mountain. They put her in jail for the night and the next day she was called up before the judge along with a bunch of drunks. When she got in front of the judge he asked what she was here for. And she said she had no idea, because she wasn't going to give him any help. The men didn't show up to charge her because this judge didn't have any jurisdiction within the Navajo boundary where she had been arrested. So the judge released her. There she was, this sixty-seven-year-old woman released sixty miles from her home, and she started to walk home. Then the policemen came along and picked her up again and took her to the right jail, but still she was never convicted or sentenced. Julian thinks that people in Washington don't know what's going on in Big Mountain, how the elders are being harassed, that this is coming from the local authorities in Flagstaff. But I doubt that; I am sure it is orchestrated in Washington.

Just then a jet flew overhead. It flew incredibly low and the whole hogan shook. We couldn't talk. I couldn't imagine any other place where a jet would be allowed to fly so low over an inhabited area. As it flew by, the coyotes screamed in terror. Catherine's sister, Pauline Whitesinger, has said that half her sheep are dead from this kind of flyover. Swan Eagle, one of the white women in the support camp, reminded me, when I asked about the flyovers, that the U.S. government is waging "techno-war" on these people, that it doesn't take a machine gun to wage war. Genocide in slow motion is more palatable.

The day before, I had interviewed Elmer Clark, a member of the Navajo-Hopi Land Commission, in his office in Flagstaff. He is a Navajo professional in his mid-thirties, obviously very concerned about the relocation problems being faced by those who have gone and those who have stayed. The Commission has been hearing testimony from the people affected by the relocation. I read the testimony of Bert Toney, a sixty-three-year-old Navajo. Bert is an Army Veteran of World War II, and his four sons are vets now, too. In his testimony, Bert says he was born and raised at Echo Canyon, the homelands from which he was relocated fourteen years ago.

> I went to World War II. I was out front at the time the war was at its peak...and I know it's very fearful. Today it seems all my sacrifice and efforts have gone unrecognized. I was told to defend my land and took the oath in

Phoenix. That's where I enlisted when I was drafted. . . .
That land (Echo Canyon) over there was our grandfather's
and it's been so for three generations. It's not something
that's only recent. Our grandfathers and grandmothers
were exiled to Fort Sumner. Many of them at that time
were massacred also. And the same thing continues today. It's no wonder you shed tears.

So it's real hard when something like this happens to
you. When the mother earth you're born on and where
your umbilical cord is buried; when the livelihood was
strong, when the cornfields flourished, where there was
no such thing as hunger; we never knew hunger when we
had livestock; sheep, horses and cattle were there to be
cared for; where water is plentiful and strong, where our
grandmother's house still stands.

Elmer Clark told me he had gone back to Echo Canyon with
Bert Toney, gone back as an archivist with his camera and tape
recorder, listening to Bert's stories about the land all the way down
the winding obscure path to the canyon floor. He showed me some
of the slides he'd taken that day, and the vistas from the canyon
rim were breathtaking. Down in the canyon were several family
hogans that had been partially bulldozed so Bert wouldn't move
back in. In one corner of the canyon, by an old corral, was a shack
that a Hopi family had built the year Bert moved out. They lived
there for two years but the place has been deserted ever since, which
is why Elmer and Bert were able to go back down the canyon.
Bert takes his canteen with him on these trips to get water from
the spring. He told Elmer that it was special water. He doesn't drink
it up in one day. Bert says it is a way to maintain his sanity. He
is in love with this area and his home, and he believes he will go
crazy if he can't have this contact with it.

The Struggle

The struggle being enacted at Big Mountain and in Central America and South Africa and with the homeless people in Times Square and other urban centers is the same. It is a struggle over how we define the sacred. For if we are willing to disbelieve the fiction that the problem at Big Mountain is between the Navajo and Hopi peoples, or that the problem in Nicaragua is between the Sandinistas and the contras, then it is possible to see that there are two opposing "sacred" forces in these and so many other places around the world. Those two forces are the "sacred" profit motive of capitalism and the sacred right of individuals to life and human dignity. But instead, just as the Reagan administration wants us to believe it is really a conflict between communism and democracy in Central America, so we are being asked to believe that these Native peoples who have lived together for (perhaps) thousands of years can no longer do so without the intervention of the United States government.

Those of us who have been to Central America know the struggle there is for something more concrete than the ideology of communism, real or imagined: it is a struggle for food, for the land reform that allows people to grow their own food, for the education that encourages free choices, and for the right to dissent without being murdered. That struggle is opposed by the corporate forces who want access to the land and other resources, access to a near-slave labor population. In the most extreme cases, achieving a profit requires genocide; there are simply too many people to feed and their labor is no longer necessary. Genocide is the result, if not the intention, of the high-intensity bombing in El Salvador's rural areas, and in Guatemala with the forced relocation of the Indian peoples. Genocide is the result, if not the intention, of Congress's Public Law 93-531 which would relocate the Hopi and Navajo peoples in the Big Mountain area.

It seems almost irrelevant to catalog the corporate interests in Big Mountain. Driving to the north, through the Black Mesa area,

I could not help but be aware of the richness under the earth; for the coal mining companies have torn the topsoil up and spilled the huge veins of coal out. Just above Tuba City I drove past an abandoned uranium processing plant with radioactive tailings open to the air. A barbed wire fence keeps the cattle and sheep out. Last year some children broke through the fence and played on the huge slag piles, unaware, of course, that they could be harmed by the radiation. Boeing owns 10 percent of Peabody Coal and Peabody owns the mineral rights to Big Mountain. As soon as the people can be forced off the land, Peabody will stripmine it; the Environmental Protection Agency has declared this desert "unreclaimable" and told Peabody Coal they don't even have to try and restore it. So this fragile ecological balance will be destroyed.

Boeing has sold enough jet airliners to South Africa to make South African Airways the aviator giant of the continent. It sells rotary blades for Huey helicopters to Central America. It provides AWAC surveillance crews and planes to advise the El Salvadoran military's bombing raids. Exxon, Bechtel, Citicorp, Chevron, Anaconda Copper all have similar patterns, involving them in the exploitation of Native people and denying those people the right to live on and possess their own lands in Africa, Central America, and the U.S. southwest. A young Navajo woman I spoke with, who was selling jewelry at Four Corners, said she wanted to own a piece of land some day that no one could take away from her. She wanted it not to belong to the tribal council and not to belong to the U.S. government, but to belong to her. "I don't think this is going to last," she said, waving her hand in the general direction of the reservation. "I think that they're starting to sell it off. They've already sold pieces of it and I just don't think this is going to be here much longer." And certainly in terms of the coal mining interests and the uranium mining interests, she is probably right.

And yet the illusion of relocation on reservation land continues. Part of Elmer Clark's job, as a Navajo-Hopi Land Commissioner, is to take families out to the New Lands to which they would be relocated if they agree to move. From October to December of 1985, the year before the relocation became mandatory, he made six trips, each time showing ten to fifteen families the potential for creating a new life. Everyone in the southwest knows about the uranium spill into a river about forty miles north of the New Lands. Residents of the nearest community have reported contamination of wells. Elmer Clark said it was the issue every family on every trip asked him about, and it is the one about which he has no information. No effort has been made to clean up the spill and no agency — none — can guarantee that the water supply to the New Lands has not been contaminated. For herders and farmers, that news means the area is essentially unusable.

In addition, the Relocation Commission has refused to recognize, or certify as eligible for Relocation funds, the extended family so central to the Navajo way of life. Generally only 50 percent of any family is certified; the other half are disqualified by stringent regulations. They are younger adults who may have chosen to live away from the family hogan for a year or so, men who have had to go to neighboring towns to work, and others. The elders, who usually do qualify, have responded by saying, "If relocation is going to happen, move my grandkids first, then my children. I want them to be accommodated, then I'll go." But the children are frequently ineligible for Relocation Funds, and so, says Clark, there is another impasse.

But the ultimate impasse may be the U.S. Congress, which has ordered the families to relocate while refusing to vote adequate funds to develop the areas into which they are to move. Clark suggested the Relocation Commission may have been responsible for drawing too grand a picture, trying to entice the families to agree to relocation at the beginning of the process. Commissioners went out to the reservation to find out what type of development — economic development, community development — they would like to see on the New Lands. Families said they wanted fire stations, police stations, senior citizens centers, preschools. And now, after all of that information gathering, families are being told that there will be no development, no community infrastructure, not even basic health-care facilities. The money available for relocation is just for housing, water, and sewers. There are no jobs to earn the money needed to pay for utilities, to build new herds, to create a life comparable to what the families are told they must abandon. It is hardly surprising the struggle for Big Mountain is bitter.

Earth As Sanctuary: The Future

Katherine Smith's youngest daughter, Mary, wants to herd sheep like her mother. She has been away from home and decided to come back. Two years studying biology at UCLA convinced her that it wasn't "relevant" so she came home. I looked around the hogan as Mary told me this, looked at the woodstove in the center of the round room where Katherine cooked, looked at the loom on one wall, the narrow beds on the other walls. I wondered what it would be like to come home to this hogan to live with no running water or electricity. What did it mean that she could make such a choice? And I had no doubt it was a choice; Mary is an intelligent, attractive, articulate young woman who could have had — I would guess — almost any career she wanted in white society. She wanted nothing it had to offer. Her mother's way of life, she was telling me, offered her everything that mattered.

Katherine Smith is one of the four keepers of the Navajo sacred earth bundles. As a white person, I have almost no idea what that means. But as a person who cares about the earth's survival, I approach Katherine Smith, keeper of the earth, with awe and reverence. And despair.

Because here is one elder woman — joined with other men and women, it is true, but they are so few — who is in opposition to all of the forces of a modern technological capitalistic society which says she is anachronistic. Life isn't that way any more, those forces say, she has to change. And Katherine Smith says no. Katherine Smith says that it is we who live in this other society who are anachronistic, that is, out of time. The earth is time, all time. She says that if we destroy the earth, we will cease to exist.

Some of the people working on Big Mountain survival issues believe that Big Mountain today is the front line, that all of the issues we have theorized about and worked for — those of us who stand for the earth — are being played out at Big Mountain: issues of how women are treated, how children are treated, how men and women can work together with mutual respect, issues of race and racism and cultural difference, and the suffering of land-based peoples all over the globe. I think they are right. I am sure that Big Mountain is one of the front lines, just as surely as Nicaragua and South Africa and Times Square are, each in its own way.

And as I drove down from Big Mountain that night in the full moonlight, the beauty of the earth and my own inability to imagine that it and its keepers could survive brought me to despair.

I wondered what it meant that as an activist I have been willing to defy the laws of my country to offer sanctuary to Central American refugees fleeing oppression in their own countries, when there is no sanctuary here in these United States for Katherine Smith and her children. What does it mean that environmentalists create sanctuaries for birds and flowers and wildlife, when there is no sanctuary in which the sacred remains of Katherine Smith's elders can be preserved and reverenced. For to walk out in any direction from her hogan on Big Mountain is to walk to a sacred place. Sometimes it is hard for a white person to recognize a sacred place, but here the earth is scattered with remnants of ancient pottery and other artifacts. Stripmining this land will destroy more than the ecology of nature; it will be a sacrilege, destroying the spiritual and material balance of Katherine Smith's world. I believe our survival in this world depends on recognizing her right to survive in a world we share.

From January, when I visited Big Mountain, until July, when I began this essay, to think about Big Mountain has been to experience over again the despair I felt that night driving down from Katherine Smith's hogan, for I am afraid the people fighting for survival at Big Mountain — their own survival and this world's survival — may not succeed. But when I went back to my notes I rediscovered a conversation I had recorded with the white woman named Swan Eagle. She had helped Pauline Whitesinger herd sheep for a number of weeks. Once Pauline had come back from a meeting with a government official who had told the people that those resisting relocation could expect to lose their lives. "Instead of getting upset," Swan Eagle reported, "Pauline told me prayers that can be said, and she said 'they work, I know. They will keep the evil away.'" For Swan Eagle, the knowledge of those prayers was a major insight into how important the ceremonies are to this struggle. "The elders," she said, "do not believe that violence on their part will win the struggle. They do believe that the unity of all the races and the shared spirituality will succeed in keeping the evil away."

It is the Navajo and Hopi elders, the traditional leaders, who are guiding the resistance at Big Mountain, and this gives me hope. White people have never before — to my knowledge — stood with Indian people when they have been facing massacre, nor have white people been willing to place themselves so completely under the direction and guidance of Indian people. It is absolutely essential, of course, that those who are being affected by the potential relocation should be allowed to set the terms of their resistance, but that has not always been the reality of solidarity work when white people have been willing to undertake it. This is, I imagine, one of the reasons the support movement for Big Mountain has been so slow to grow: that absolute insistence that anyone coming into the Navajo/Hopi cultures be willing to recognize and honor and take direction from the leaders of those cultures. What will be special for the white person who can enter into the space at Big Mountain in a supportive way will be the gift of directly sharing the danger and oppression of the Indian resisters.

As I drove away from the reservation, I saw a Navajo man in a wheelchair hitchhiking by the side of the road, going the opposite way from me. He sat in the wheelchair, his face impassive, his arm out to wave down any willing driver. He was close to my age and I imagine he was a Vietnam veteran. He had lost the use of his legs. Perhaps he was about to lose his home to the strip-miners. And I wondered how much more he would lose in the struggle to survive. Bert Toney's grandparents were massacred; other Indians were exiled to Fort Sumner. The same thing continues today, Bert said, and he is right.

It's no wonder you shed tears.

From Big Mountain

If you believed the land is holy
  the earth has heartbeat and breath
if you knew where your umbilical cord
  had been buried at your birth
    tethering you in its circumference
and which pinyon tree had given a branch
  for your cradle board
where lightning has struck
where the rocks speak to you
where blue larkspur pollen has been sprinkled
  to sanctify
where a coyote crossed your path
where the spruce was asked to protect you
  the first day you went into strange lands
    away from this circumference of natural protection
where cornmeal bread was baked
  in the belly of the earth
    when you became a woman
if you believed yourself known by the hills
  by the canyons
    by the buffalo grass
      by the streams and rivers
as you are known by your mother or sister or son
  touched and shaped
each by each

what would allow you to understand
this nation of immigrants rushing
from our birthplaces to unknown
destinies in cities so far removed
from the earth that trees and streams
are invisible? how could I tell you
what was given to me as a child —
a dream shaped by struggle
a dream called progress
the belief that life will be better
for my children...not the same
certainly not the same
as my parents and grandparents.

If you believed the land is holy
you would understand the long journeys
  begun when the land said no
    when the water source failed
      when the earth was sterile from too much providing
as the Anasazi people went out from Chaco Canyon
  and the Hohokam
    known only as "those who have gone"
      left their terraced garden plots
so my immigrant grandparents left in times of famine
when the potato harvest failed
  when there was drought or too much rain
    when there was no land to farm or graze

and you would understand
  when they fled in fear
    fled pogroms
    and debtor's prison
    and the flame
    the noose
as you fled and are still fleeing.

But if you believed the land is holy
  you — reading or hearing this poem —
if you knew yourself a keeper of the earth
called upon by your grandparents
to protect the earth from invasion
  to allow no one to tear her skin
    destroy her heart that beats under La Plata
      her lungs breathing through the ridges of Mount Taylor
and if you believed the people too are inscribed in the land
  tears and sweat mingling with the waters
    every prayer breathed a part of the living air
      a spirit returned to the people with the harvest of corn

how could you image the casual
relocation of human communities
to make room for a highway
a dam or a railroad or know
how the words *right of way*
came to mean the right of a truck?

But I — who was shaped by this dream
and a sharp necessity no less real
than the hidden contours of the land
that shapes your children —
I must now ask myself
if I believe the land is holy

what distance must I travel
  what must I venture
    what must I risk
how much time is left to answer?

Today

this is her life. She makes coffee in the morning
from beans she grinds herself. Some mornings she sits on
a porch where the only sound is birdsong. Other days
the traffic growls by as commuters go to work. Some days

she can go to her desk and answer letters and write
about her work and where she has been and what
she is thinking about where she has been. Other days she

becomes a commuter and goes to an office and reads what
other people have written about their lives and work. She
corrects their grammar and helps them organize their
thoughts. She tries not to write their lives for them.

Some days she hears the words coming at her from newspapers and televisions and she feels nearly insane with
grief. On other days there are no words and she wanders

through the meadow, knee deep in clover and thistle, not
even letting the words in her mind. Sometimes after
a day like that she can let the words back in and they
come orderly to the page, but more often than she would like

they rush back over the smooth rocks of calm she had
stored so carefully, and on the page she finds only words,
no meaning. Then she remembers that she is the woman who

walks through the pasture and looks at the flowers and
that she is the woman who can love the flowers without
naming them or identifying them. And sometimes this helps
the words to come again, describing each thing as it is,

seeing each detail with her heart.

Other titles from Firebrand Books include:

Beneath My Heart, Poetry by Janice Gould/$8.95

The Big Mama Stories by Shay Youngblood/$8.95

A Burst Of Light, Essays by Audre Lorde/$7.95

Crime Against Nature, Poetry by Minnie Bruce Pratt/$8.95

Diamonds Are A Dyke's Best Friend by Yvonne Zipter/$9.95

Dykes To Watch Out For, Cartoons by Alison Bechdel/$6.95

Exile In The Promised Land, A Memoir by Marcia Freedman/$8.95

Eye Of A Hurricane, Stories by Ruthann Robson / $8.95

The Fires Of Bride, A Novel by Ellen Galford/$8.95

A Gathering Of Spirit, A Collection by North American Indian Women edited by Beth Brant *(Degonwadonti)*/$9.95

Getting Home Alive by Aurora Levins Morales and Rosario Morales /$8.95

Good Enough To Eat, A Novel by Lesléa Newman/$8.95

Humid Pitch, Narrative Poetry by Cheryl Clarke/$8.95

Jewish Women's Call For Peace edited by Rita Falbel, Irena Klepfisz, and Donna Nevel/$4.95

Jonestown & Other Madness, Poetry by Pat Parker/$7.95

Just Say Yes, A Novel by Judith McDaniel/$8.95

The Land Of Look Behind, Prose and Poetry by Michelle Cliff/$6.95

A Letter To Harvey Milk, Short Stories by Lesléa Newman/$8.95

Letting In The Night, A Novel by Joan Lindau/$8.95

Living As A Lesbian, Poetry by Cheryl Clarke/$7.95

Making It, A Woman's Guide to Sex in the Age of AIDS by Cindy Patton and Janis Kelly/$4.95

Metamorphosis, Reflections On Recovery, by Judith McDaniel/$7.95

Mohawk Trail by Beth Brant *(Degonwadonti)*/$7.95

Moll Cutpurse, A Novel by Ellen Galford/$7.95

More Dykes To Watch Out For, Cartoons by Alison Bechdel/$7.95

The Monarchs Are Flying, A Novel by Marion Foster/$8.95

(continued)

Movement In Black, Poetry by Pat Parker/$8.95

My Mama's Dead Squirrel, Lesbian Essays on Southern Culture by Mab Segrest/$8.95

New, Improved! Dykes To Watch Out For, Cartoons by Alison Bechdel/$7.95

The Other Sappho, A Novel by Ellen Frye/$8.95

Politics Of The Heart, A Lesbian Parenting Anthology edited by Sandra Pollack and Jeanne Vaughn/$11.95

Presenting...Sister NoBlues by Hattie Gossett/$8.95

A Restricted Country by Joan Nestle/$8.95

Sacred Space by Geraldine Hatch Hanon/$9.95

Sans Souci, And Other Stories by Dionne Brand/$8.95

Scuttlebutt, A Novel by Jana Williams/$8.95

Shoulders, A Novel by Georgia Cotrell/$8.95

Simple Songs, Stories by Vickie Sears/$8.95

The Sun Is Not Merciful, Short Stories by Anna Lee Walters/$7.95

Tender Warriors, A Novel by Rachel Guido deVries/$8.95

This Is About Incest by Margaret Randall/$7.95

The Threshing Floor, Short Stories by Barbara Burford/$7.95

Trash, Stories by Dorothy Allison/$8.95

The Women Who Hate Me, Poetry by Dorothy Allison/$8.95

Words To The Wise, A Writer's Guide to Feminist and Lesbian Periodicals & Publishers by Andrea Fleck Clardy/$4.95

Yours In Struggle, Three Feminist Perspectives on Anti-Semitism and Racism by Elly Bulkin, Minnie Bruce Pratt, and Barbara Smith/$8.95

You can buy Firebrand titles at your bookstore, or order them directly from the publisher (141 The Commons, Ithaca, New York 14850, 607-272-0000).

Please include $2.00 shipping for the first book and $.50 for each additional book.

A free catalog is available on request.